ReadyGEN

Text Collection

GRADE 4

PEARSON

Glenview, Illinois • Boston, Massachusetts • Chandler, Arizona • Hoboken, New Jersey

Cover: Huguette Pizzic

ISBN-13: 978-0-328-85282-6
ISBN-10: 0-328-85282-1
4 5 6 7 8 9 10 V003 19 18 17 16

Table of Contents

Unit 1 Becoming Researchers

Unit 2 Exploring Culture and Nature

Fragile Frogs

The Frog Scientist

BY PAMELA S. TURNER

Amphibian scientists are like everybody else. They like to talk about what they do. At an international conference in 1989, nearly everyone was telling the same story. There seemed to be fewer amphibians (frogs, toads, salamanders, and caecilians). Each scientist thought it was happening just to the animals he or she studied. But when the scientists talked to one another, they realized it was happening everywhere.

Concerned scientists surveyed amphibian populations all over the world. They discovered that about a third of amphibians (1,856 out of 5,743 species) are threatened with extinction. Since 1980 at least 122 species have probably become extinct.

Australia had a remarkable species called the gastric brooding frog. The mother frog swallowed her eggs and hatched her babies in her stomach. The little frogs hopped from their mother's mouth into the big wide world. During the 1980s, the Australian gastric brooding frogs disappeared.

Amphibian means "double life." Most amphibians begin their life in a watery world, breathing through fishlike gills. Then they transform into an entirely different creature: an air-breathing animal.

RED-LEGGED WALKING FROG

Something similar happened in Costa Rica. Golden toads once lived in Costa Rica's cool, wet forests. The males of the two-inch-long species were golden orange, like web-footed tangerines. They gathered by the hundreds during breeding season. The golden toad was last seen in 1989. Like the gastric brooding frog, the golden toad is now considered extinct. No one knows what killed the gastric brooding frogs or the golden toads.

Habitat loss is a big problem for many wild animals, including amphibians. Frogs, toads, and salamanders die when wetlands are drained, ponds are filled, or forests are cut down. Sometimes amphibian habitat is fragmented (chopped into smaller pieces) when roads, houses, or shopping centers are built. Imagine a tiny frog trying to hop safely across a freeway or parking lot.

Scientists looked closely at places where amphibians were declining. To their surprise, they found it wasn't always where habitat was being lost or fragmented. Frogs were disappearing from protected areas, or places very far from humans. Costa Rica's golden toad lived in a national park. The gastric brooding frog lived in remote parts of Australia.

ABOVE
This red-legged walking frog from Africa looks like he's wearing tiger-striped underwear. Walking frogs take steps with their hind legs instead of hopping.

RIGHT
The only golden toads left are museum specimens like this one. The species is believed to be extinct.

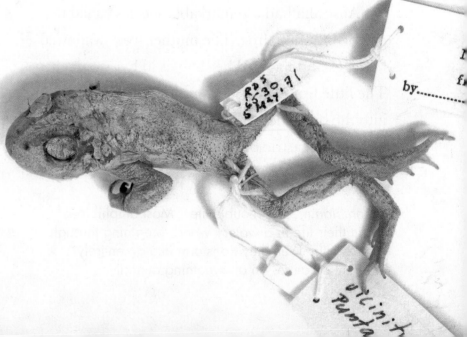

SONORAN
DESERT TOAD

Deformed frogs appeared, too. In 1995, middle school students in Minnesota found some frogs near a farm. They were juvenile leopard frogs, just like the ones Tyrone studies. Many of the Minnesota frogs had missing legs, or shriveled legs, or legs that didn't bend. It was strange and scary. People began finding deformed frogs in many other places, too.

What is happening to the world's amphibians?

The answer isn't simple. Amphibian decline has many causes. Since the 1980s the chytrid (pronounced *KIT-rid*) fungus has spread around the world. The disease is killing amphibians in North America, Central America, South America, and Australia. To make matters worse, global warming seems to cause temperatures that help the fungus

A deadly fungus that threatens frogs was first discovered in the blue poison dart frog (above) and White's tree frog (shown on page 9).

LEFT Blue poison dart frogs live in South America.

BELOW This leopard frog was caught by a child in Reedsburg, Wisconsin. It has an extra leg growing out of its chin. Other deformed frogs were found in the same place.

spread. Though scientists in New Zealand believe they've discovered a chemical that kills the fungus, finding and treating wild frogs would be very difficult.

Some species of frogs living at high altitudes are threatened by ultraviolet (UV) radiation. Man-made chemicals have thinned the ozone layer in our atmosphere. The earth's ozone layer keeps most of these damaging UV rays from reaching us. At high altitudes the air is thinner, and if thin air is combined with a thin ozone area, even more UV radiation reaches the earth. High levels of UV radiation can kill the delicate, shell-less eggs of amphibians that live in mountain areas.

Amphibians are also threatened by introduced species. An introduced species is a creature that shows up somewhere it isn't normally found. The bullfrog, a kind of frog that *isn't* declining, is native to the eastern and midwestern parts of the United States. It has been introduced by humans into ponds and streams all over the West. Introduced bullfrogs gobble up smaller native frogs and take over their habitat. Sometimes fish are introduced into lakes and streams so fisherman will have something to catch. The non-native fish usually have a taste for the native tadpoles.

Often a frog species faces not just one threat but many. California's red-legged frog has been hit by a truckload of problems: habitat loss, fungal disease, and introduced bullfrogs and fish. And if all that weren't enough, red-legged frogs are also killed by pesticides sprayed on crops in California's Central Valley. The pesticides are blown by the wind into the foothills where many of the remaining frogs live.

White's tree frog is found in Australia.

AMERICAN
BULLFROG

And those scary frog deformities? Scientists found that some frog deformities are caused by a parasite. The parasite is a worm that burrows under a tadpole's skin and disrupts the tadpole's growth. It may prevent a leg from growing or cause deformed legs.

Pesticides such as atrazine make frogs more vulnerable to parasites. And pesticides can also cause strange frog deformities. Sometimes those deformities aren't as obvious as missing or shriveled legs. Yet hidden deformities can still harm frogs. That's what Tyrone found when he tested frogs exposed to atrazine.

OPPOSITE

Bullfrogs are very aggressive and prey on other frogs. Like all amphibians, bullfrogs are cold-blooded. That means the temperature inside their body changes as the outside temperature changes.

BELOW

A Bell's horned frog gulps down a newborn mouse below. It is sometimes called the Pac Man frog after the munching video game creature. Instead of chasing its prey, the Pac Man sits and waits like a web-footed couch potato.

Movers & Shapers

by Dr. Patricia Macnair

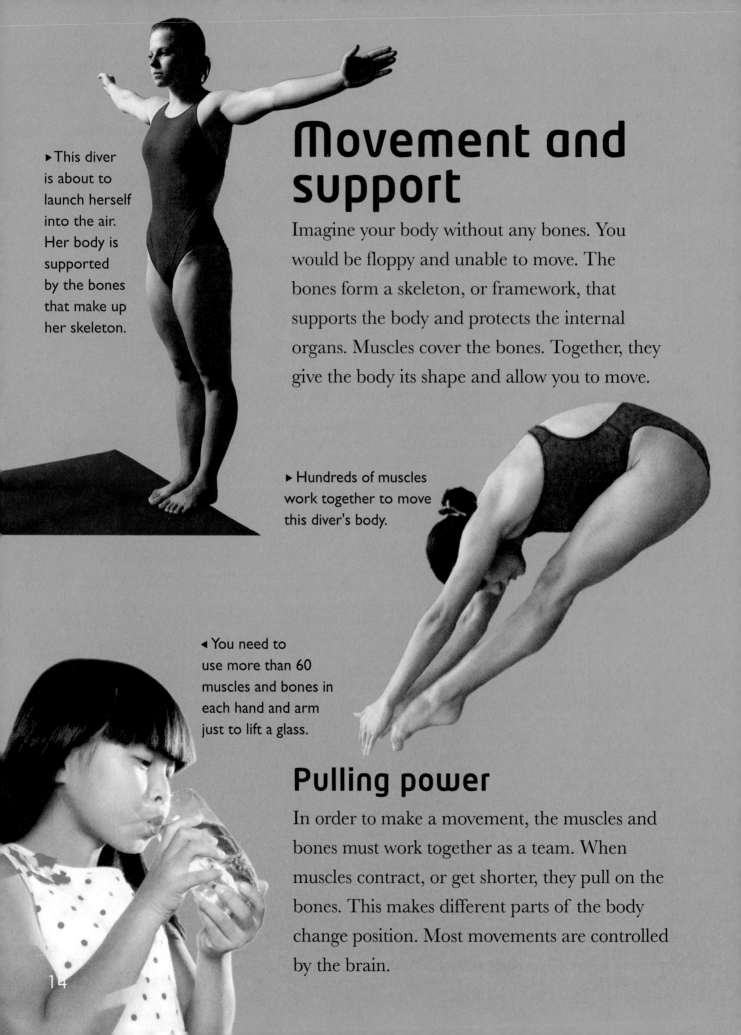

▶ This diver is about to launch herself into the air. Her body is supported by the bones that make up her skeleton.

Movement and support

Imagine your body without any bones. You would be floppy and unable to move. The bones form a skeleton, or framework, that supports the body and protects the internal organs. Muscles cover the bones. Together, they give the body its shape and allow you to move.

▶ Hundreds of muscles work together to move this diver's body.

◀ You need to use more than 60 muscles and bones in each hand and arm just to lift a glass.

Pulling power

In order to make a movement, the muscles and bones must work together as a team. When muscles contract, or get shorter, they pull on the bones. This makes different parts of the body change position. Most movements are controlled by the brain.

No rest

Your muscles and bones never stop working. Even when you are standing still, they are busy holding the body in the same position. And all day and night the muscles and bones in your rib cage move in order to help you breathe.

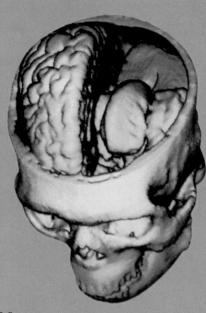

▶ This picture, called a CAT scan, shows the inside of a person's head. The bones of the skull protect the brain. The left-hand side of the brain is not shown in this scan.

▼ During a dive the muscles pull on the bones. This makes the body bend or straighten.

Guard duty

Bones and muscles also have the important job of protecting the organs inside your body. The skull forms a hard cage around the brain. Your ribs shield the heart and lungs, and the bones and muscles of the pelvis protect the bladder and reproductive organs.

▼ To stand at attention, these soldiers are using muscles in their necks, backs, and legs.

Info lab

■ A bone is stronger than a steel bar that is the same weight.

■ More than half of the bones in your body are found in your hands and feet.

■ Muscles are grouped in pairs.

■ Muscles make up around half of the weight of your body.

Bony framework

The skeleton is made up of bones of all shapes and sizes. Arm and leg bones are long and thin, while hand bones are small and rounded. Although bones are hard and rigid, they can grow and change their shape.

▼ Long bones—such as the femur, or thighbone—are filled with marrow. The blood vessels provide bone cells with food and oxygen.

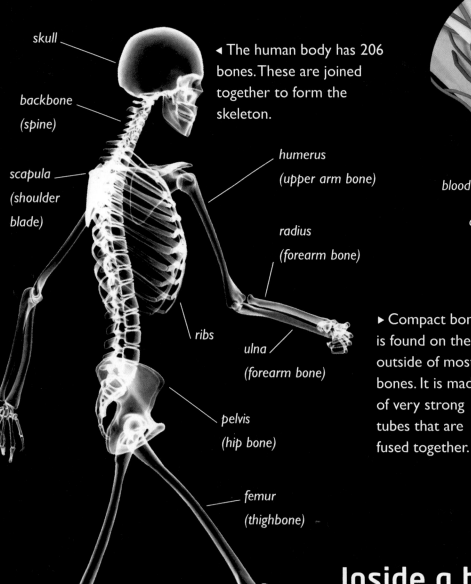

skull

backbone (spine)

scapula (shoulder blade)

◄ The human body has 206 bones. These are joined together to form the skeleton.

humerus (upper arm bone)

radius (forearm bone)

ribs

ulna (forearm bone)

pelvis (hip bone)

femur (thighbone)

patella (kneecap)

tibia (shinbone)

tarsals (anklebones)

blood vessel

compact bone

spongy bone

bone marrow

► Compact bone is found on the outside of most bones. It is made of very strong tubes that are fused together.

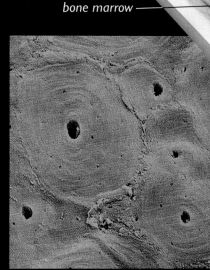

Inside a bone

The surface of each bone is covered with a thin layer containing blood vessels and nerves. Underneath is hard bone called compact bone. This forms a shell around a layer of light but very strong spongy bone.

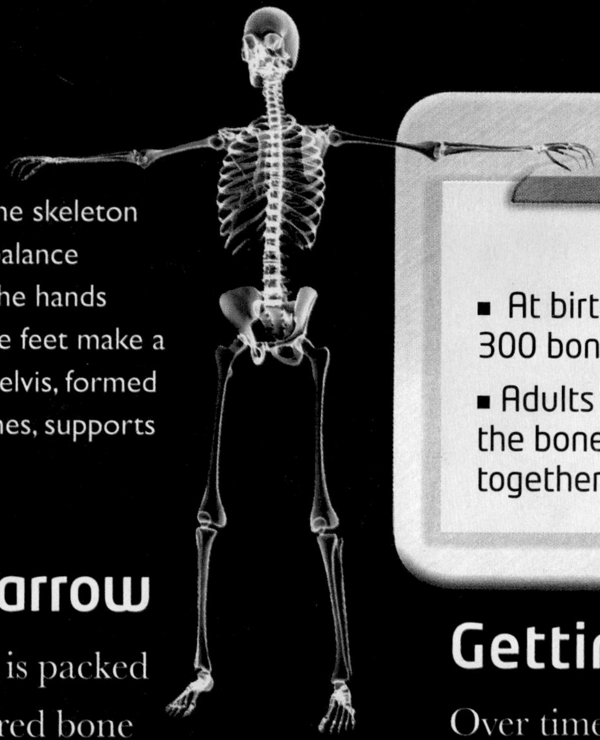

▶ The shape of the skeleton helps the body balance upright, leaving the hands free. Bones in the feet make a wide base. The pelvis, formed from the hip bones, supports the upper body.

Bone marrow

Spongy bone is packed with jellylike red bone marrow. This is where blood cells are made. As a child grows into an adult, the red bone marrow in long bones is replaced by yellow bone marrow, which stores fat.

spongy bone

Getting it right

Over time bones can change their shape because they are made of millions of living cells. This is why it is very important to have your feet measured when you buy shoes. Shoes that are too tight can damage the bones of your feet.

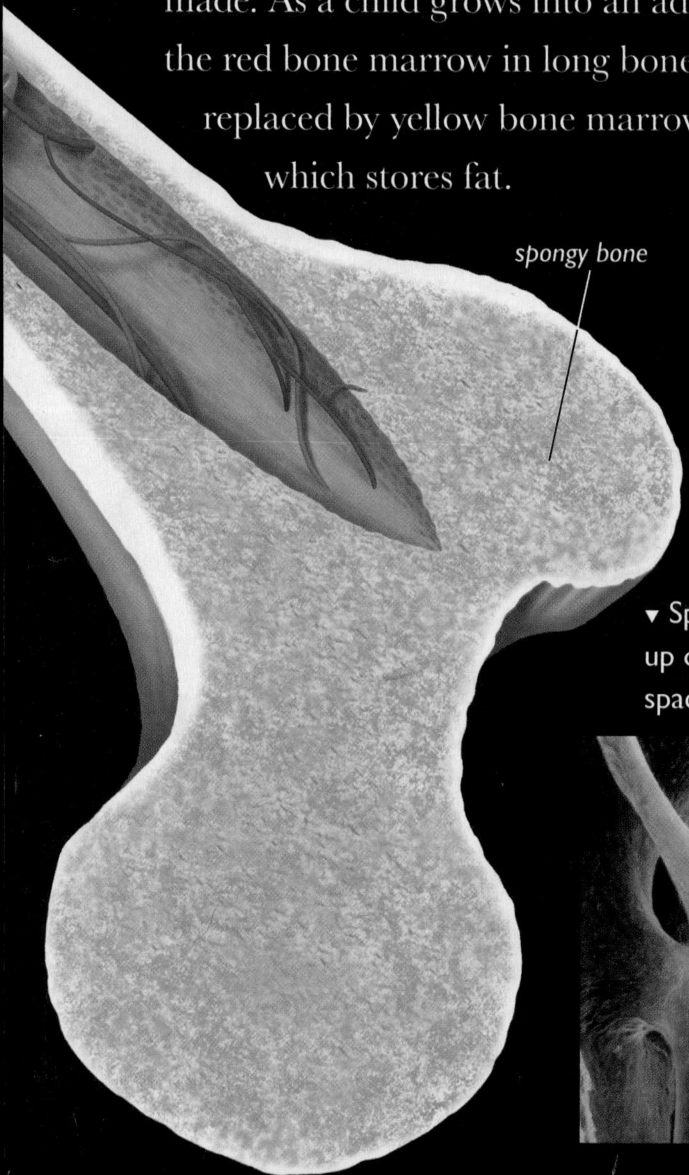

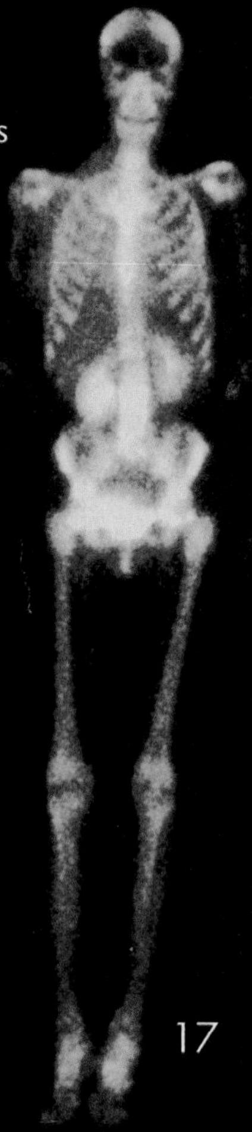

▶ Special scans can detect if the bones of a living person are diseased. This picture shows a healthy skeleton.

▼ Spongy bone is not solid; it is made up of a network of bony struts. The spaces are filled with bone marrow.

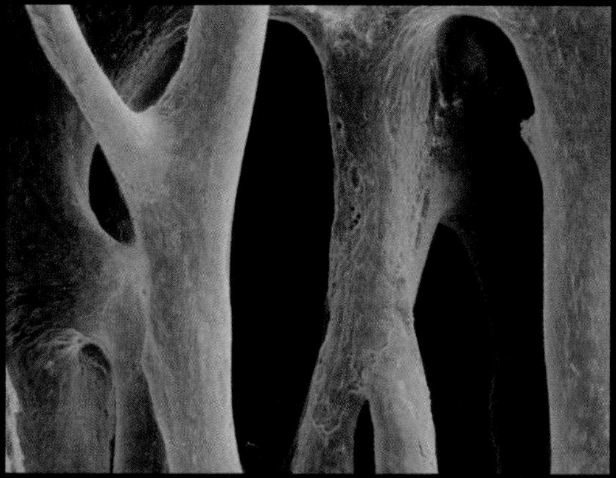

The joints

Wherever two or more bones meet, you will find a joint. In some joints the bones are fixed tightly together. In others the bones can move freely, allowing different parts of the body to bend or twist. Without this flexibility, it would be almost impossible for you to move.

Smooth operators

Joints have to work smoothly in order to prevent wear and tear. In joints like the knee the bone ends have a slippery coating called cartilage. A fluid in between the layers of cartilage stops the bones from rubbing together.

▼ This picture was taken with an endoscope. It shows the cartilage inside a knee joint.

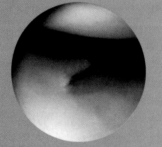

▼ Joints and other parts of the body can be examined with a special instrument called an endoscope.

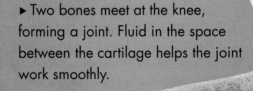

▶ Two bones meet at the knee, forming a joint. Fluid in the space between the cartilage helps the joint work smoothly.

pelvis (hip bone)

femur (thigh bone)

fluid

cartilage

Chain of bones

Your spine is often called the backbone, but if it was just one stiff bone, you would be unable to bend over. Instead it is made up of many vertebrae, or small bones, with narrow joints in between each one of them.

▼ The joints between each vertebra of the spine can move slightly apart.

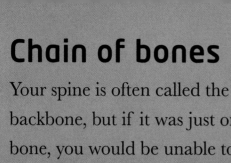

vertebra

joint

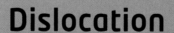

▶ This X-ray shows a dislocated knuckle or finger joint. You can see how the two bones have been pushed apart.

Dislocation

Bones are held very tightly in place at each joint by tough bands called ligaments. If a bone is knocked hard enough, it may move out of place. This is called a dislocation, and the joint will not bend correctly until the bone is put back into the right place.

How joints move

Joints move in many different ways. Some joints work like a hinge—bend your knee to see this in action. Others, such as the shoulder, let you make movements in many directions.

Ball and socket

Your hip and shoulder are examples of ball-and- socket joints. One bone rotates just like a ball that is inside a cuplike socket formed by another bone. Ball-and-socket joints are the most movable of all joints.

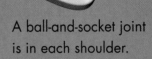

A ball-and-socket joint is in each shoulder.

Hinges and pivots

The knee, elbow, fingers, and toes contain hinge joints. These move backward and forward in only one direction. The elbow also contains a pivot joint, which lets you turn your hand over and then back again.

▼ If a hip joint becomes diseased, it can be replaced with an artificial joint made out of metal (shown in red).

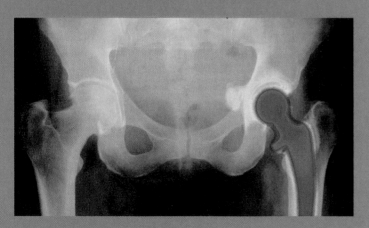

Info lab

■ People with "double joints" do not have extra joints—they are just more flexible.

■ Every step you take involves the 33 joints in each of your feet.

■ In some of the ankle and wrist joints the bones glide over each other.

The saddle joint is only found in the hands.

The pivot joint at the top of the spine allows the head to turn.

▲ This performer can twist and turn her body into this shape because she has very flexible joints.

Thumb power

The saddle joint is found at the base of the thumb. This joint lets you move each thumb in a wide circle. Along with your fingers, your thumbs help you grip objects in your hands.

Flexibility

A hinge joint is found in the knees.

Imagine being able to put your feet behind your ears! Some people have extremely flexible joints, so they can bend their bodies into unusual and extreme positions.

◄The body has several different types of joints. Each one allows a different movement, from bending a knee to moving an arm in a circle.

Bendable body parts

Try folding your ears forward. They should bend easily and then spring back when you let go! This happens because they are made of a flexible tissue called cartilage. Your nose and voice box, which is the bumpy part in your neck, also contain cartilage.

On the nose

Your nose is made of several pieces of cartilage. They form the sides of your nose and give your nostrils their shape. A central piece of cartilage, called the septum, divides the inside of the nose into two chambers.

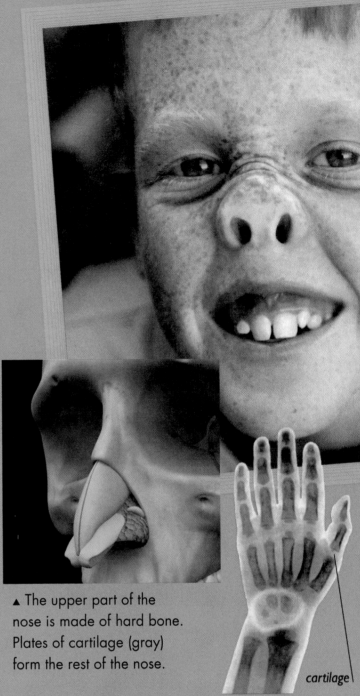

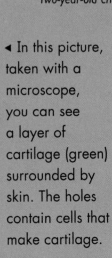

▲ The upper part of the nose is made of hard bone. Plates of cartilage (gray) form the rest of the nose.

cartilage

Two-year-old child

▼ Cartilage is soft enough for an earring to be pierced through it.

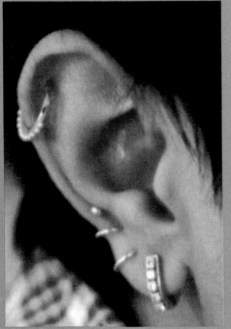

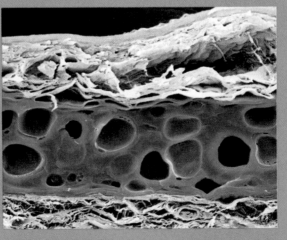

◄ In this picture, taken with a microscope, you can see a layer of cartilage (green) surrounded by skin. The holes contain cells that make cartilage.

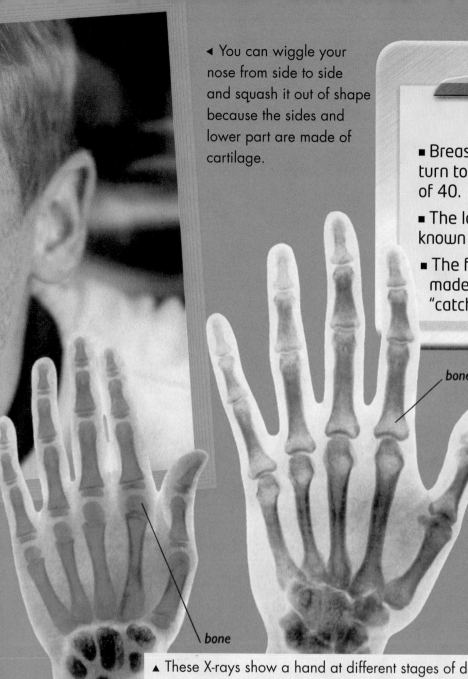

◄ You can wiggle your nose from side to side and squash it out of shape because the sides and lower part are made of cartilage.

bone

Soft skeleton

For the first six weeks a baby developing in its mother's womb has a skeleton made of cartilage. Cartilage is softer and more flexible than bone and grows and changes more quickly.

bone

▲ These X-rays show a hand at different stages of development. By the time adulthood is reached, the cartilage (lighter areas) has been replaced by bone (blue)

Seven-year-old child

Adult

Growth and repair

Cartilage is easily damaged, especially in the knee joints. Many athletes have to retire because of cartilage injuries. But scientists are now able to grow new cartilage in laboratories, giving hope to injured athletes.

Cartilage into bone

In young children the bones still contain large areas of cartilage in between more rigid bone. These pieces of cartilage are called growth plates— because they let bones grow. Over time most cartilage is replaced by bone.

Muscles that get you moving

Without muscles, you would not be able to scratch your head, open a door, or turn a single page of this book! The muscles you use for these and most other movements are joined to the bones. Muscles work by pulling on the bones.

Under the skin

There are almost 650 muscles in your body that you can control and move. This type of muscle, called skeletal muscle, is connected firmly to the bones by tough, stringlike cords. These cords are the tendons.

This muscle wrinkles your forehead

Chest muscles pull the arm forward

This muscle twists the body

This thigh muscle straightens the knees

▶ Underneath your skin are hundreds of overlapping muscles. Most are attached to your skeleton.

▲ ▶ Muscle is made from long muscle cells, called fibers, packed together in bundles (right). Under a microscope, these fibers look striped (above).

The trapezius muscle pulls the head and shoulders back

The deltoid muscle raises the arms

The buttocks muscle straightens the thighs

The calf muscle bends the feet down

How muscles work

Muscles move the body because they are attached to the skeleton. When a muscle contracts, it gets shorter and pulls on a bone. Try bending an arm. If you put your hand on the upper part of your arm, you should feel the muscle become fatter as it gets shorter.

Muscle pairs

The muscles we use for movement are controlled and coordinated by the brain. Most muscles work in pairs. One pulls in one direction, and the other pulls in the opposite direction.

◀ ▼ The biceps muscle near the front of each upper arm bends the arm up at the elbow. The triceps, at the back, straightens out the arm.

The skull

The skull is like a hard box made of bone. It contains and protects the brain and other soft body parts, such as the eyes, ears, and tongue, which can be damaged easily. Nerves and blood vessels go in and out from the brain through holes in the skull.

Bone head

The skull is formed from 22 bones. Eight of these are large, flat bones that make up a domed box called the cranium. This surrounds the brain. The remaining bones give shape to the face. Only one skull bone can move— the mandible, or jawbone.

Balancing act

The bones of the cranium fit together very tightly and cannot move or slip unless the skull is hit with great force. The skull is balanced on top of the backbone. The spinal cord runs along the backbone and into the brain through a large opening at the base of the skull.

▲ This decorated skull mask is used during the Mexican Day of the Dead festival. Ancestors are remembered and celebrated on this day.

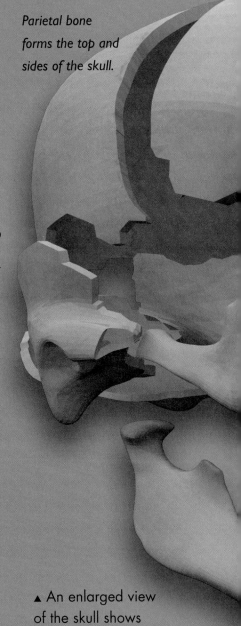

Parietal bone forms the top and sides of the skull.

▲ An enlarged view of the skull shows how the bones fit together like a jigsaw puzzle. The jagged edges lock the bones into place.

▲ This cyclist is taking no chances. A helmet protects his skull and brain from knocks and falls.

Frontal bone forms the forehead.

zygomatic bone (cheekbone)

Info lab
- The bones around the nose are hollow in order to keep the skull as light as possible.
- The fontanels of a baby become bone between the age of 12 and 18 months old.

maxilla (upper jaw)

mandible (lower jaw)

Safety first

Although the skull is strong, sometimes it needs extra help in order to protect its precious contents. In many sports, such as cycling, skateboarding, or football, it is important to wear protective headgear.

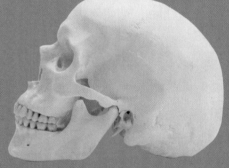

▲ The jawbone is the strongest and largest bone in the skull. You use it to chew food and to help you speak.

▲ At the front of the skull there are two large openings called orbits. These hold the eyes.

Fontanels

In small babies the bones of the skull have not yet knitted together. Instead the bones are connected by a stretchy material. The gaps between the bones are called fontanels. These allow the skull to get bigger as the baby's brain grows.

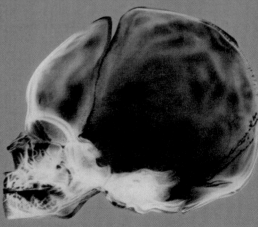

▲ This X-ray of the side of a baby's skull shows the fontanels, or gaps, that close up as the skull grows.

27

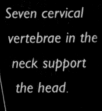

Spine and ribs

Feel the bumps running down the middle of your back. Each one is a ringlike bone called a vertebra. These bones form the spine, or backbone, which is the central part of the skeleton. Twelve pairs of curved rib bones are also attached to the spine.

Seven cervical vertebrae in the neck support the head.

▶ The ribs curve around the chest on both sides of the spine. Most are connected to the sternum, or breastbone, at the front.

Support system

The spine is made up of curved sections. Each one has a different job to do, from supporting the head to carrying the weight of your body. The different sections of the spine together form a gentle "S" shape. This helps make the spine flexible and strong.

Twelve thoracic vertebrae are connected to your ribs.

◀ ▲ The spine has 33 bones—24 separate vertebrae and nine that are fused together.

▼ Here part of the vertebrae has broken off in an accident and is pressing against the spinal cord.

Five large lumbar vertebrae support most of your body weight.

These five fused vertebrae form the sacrum, which secures the spine to the pelvis.

Four fused vertebrae form the coccyx, or tailbone.

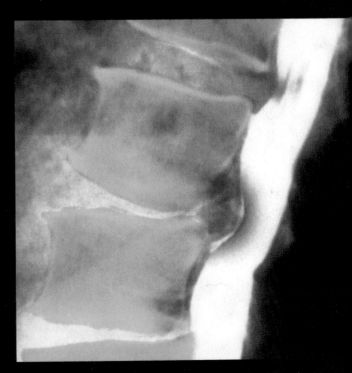

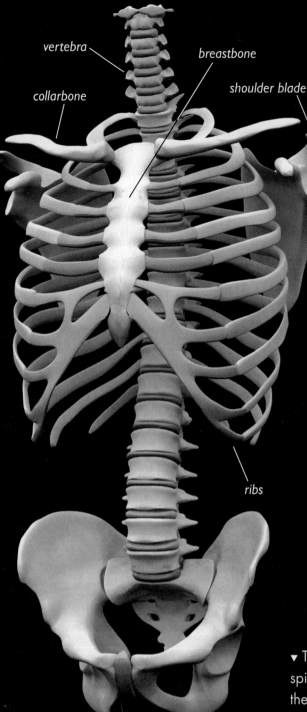

vertebra

collarbone

breastbone

shoulder blade

ribs

The ribs

The ribs form a protective cage around your lungs and heart. When you breathe, your rib cage moves up and down, helping your lungs suck in air and squeeze it out again.

▼ The atlas is found at the top of the spine. This vertebra, along with the one below it, allows you to shake and nod your head.

Antishock

When you move, stand, or jump, you put pressure on your spine. Between each vertebra there are padded disks of cartilage. These cushion and protect the bones of the spine from damage.

▶ The atlas, which supports your head, is named after a character from one of the myths of ancient Greece. This sculpture shows Atlas carrying Earth on his shoulders.

Legs and feet

When you are walking, running, or just standing still, your legs and feet have to carry the weight of your whole body. The femur, or thighbone, in the upper part of the leg, is connected to the body by the pelvis. The femur is the largest and strongest bone in the body.

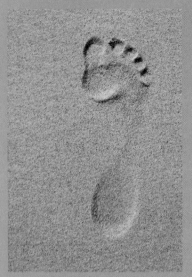

▲ Look at a footprint and you can see that the sole is not flat. Arches of bone raise the inner part of the foot off the ground.

tibia (shinbone)

femur (thighbone)

Bone basin

The basin-shaped pelvis is where the upper and lower body meet. The pelvis is made from two curved hip bones joined together at the front. At the back the hip bones are connected to the backbone.

Under pressure

When you are moving, your feet push your body forward. They also stop you from falling over! The bones and ligaments of the foot form curves called arches. These can bend under the weight of the body, and they turn the feet into excellent shock absorbers.

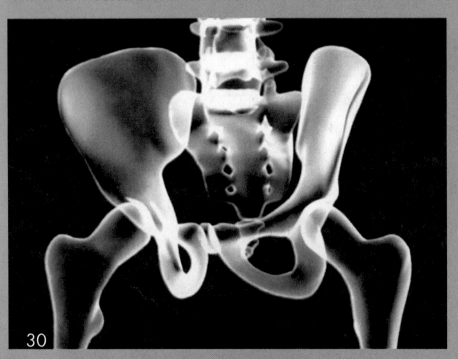

◄ The legs are joined to the spine by the pelvis. The pelvis also surrounds the reproductive and digestive organs.

All in a name

The sartorius muscle is the longest muscle in the body. Found in the thigh, it is around 1 ft. (30cm) long and pulls the knee up and rotates the thigh outward. The sartorius also lets you sit cross-legged. Ancient Roman tailors, called sartors, sat like this when they sewed.

Info lab

- There are 26 bones, 33 joints, and more than 100 muscles, tendons, and ligaments in each foot.

- The muscles of your feet expand slightly during the day.

- The bones and muscles of the arms and legs are very similar.

sartorius muscle

◄ Bones and muscles in our legs and arms support the body everyday. This gymnast uses both his arms and legs as he performs his gymnastic routine.

▲ A runner winces in pain after injuring her ankle.

tarsals (anklebones)   metatarsals (sole bones)   phalanges (toe bones)

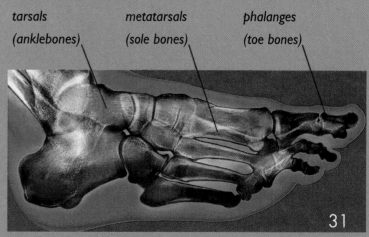

► Each foot contains seven tarsals, or anklebones, five metatarsals, or sole bones, and 14 phalanges, or toe bones.

31

KING OF THE PARKING LOT

PARKING LOT

BY GABY TRIANA

PHILIPPA LANGLEY IS A WOMAN ON A MISSION.

As a modern-day screenwriter and history fan, Philippa's favorite topic to study is Richard III, one of the most famous kings in England's history. This legendary king, who died over 500 years ago, had quite the bad reputation. After his brief two-year reign and death in 1485, he is remembered for being a cruel killer. William Shakespeare wrote a play about him in 1592 titled *Richard III* and described him as a cold-hearted, selfish villain. Paintings created after his death portray him with narrowed eyes, a hunched back, and even clawed fingers.

But Philippa knew that every story has two sides. Had Richard III really been the bad guy everyone said? Or did the following rulers of England just make him seem that way to make themselves look good? Could Philippa possibly find his missing remains and even clues about the king's real personality so long after his death?

Many experts said that locating him would be impossible.

But Philippa had a dream—to find the long lost king.

Portrait of Richard III

LOST AND FOUND

Modern scientists can tell a lot about people who lived long ago by studying their remains. However, there was no body or skeleton of Richard III anywhere to be found. Some records said he was buried at the Greyfriars Church in Leicester, England, after he died at the Battle of Bosworth in 1485. However, some said that his body was removed and thrown into the River Soar after King Henry VII tore down Greyfriars Church.

Philippa Langley is a member of The Richard III Society. This group studies everything about King Richard III. They believed he might still be buried at the site of that old church. But where exactly was that? If Philippa could locate where the church used to be, she could dig and hopefully locate his missing buried bones.

36

Philippa raised money and got a license to start an excavation to dig. She hired archaeologists and scientists who found an old map of Leicester. This map showed a possible location of the Greyfriars Church. They laid the old map on top of a current map of Leicester and discovered something. The old church used to sit in an area that was now a parking lot between two office buildings. Could the king still be there after all these years?

On September 8, 2012, Philippa and her team began digging to find out.

WHAT THEY FOUND

For four days, archaeologists dug two long trenches under the surface of the parking lot. Immediately, they found walls and floors of a building that may have once belonged to a monastery, a place where monks lived and prayed. This was exciting, since it was said that when Richard III died in battle, monks took his body away on a horse.

Philippa and her team grew more excited. Their next plan was to find the church inside of the friary, and after that, the choir within the church. If they could find the choir, they would look underneath it, where sources said the remains of the missing king might lay if he were still buried.

After only four days, one of the archaeologists found something else buried under the choir in an area called "the walking place." Many years ago, it was tradition for important people to be buried under floor areas where many people walked, as a sign of respect. The archaeologist immediately called in more team members to look at it.

One of them, Jo Appleby, a bone expert, began removing dirt and made an amazing discovery—a human skeleton was under the floor. As she worked to uncover it, two things made her stare in disbelief. First, the size and shape of the bones. By looking at the shoulders and pelvis, she could see it once belonged to a human adult male. Even more amazing, its spine was curved in the shape of a "C" in the middle. Whoever the skeleton belonged to, his back was once deformed. Jo Appleby knew that Richard III was rumored to be a hunchback, so she called Philippa Langley to show her what she had found.

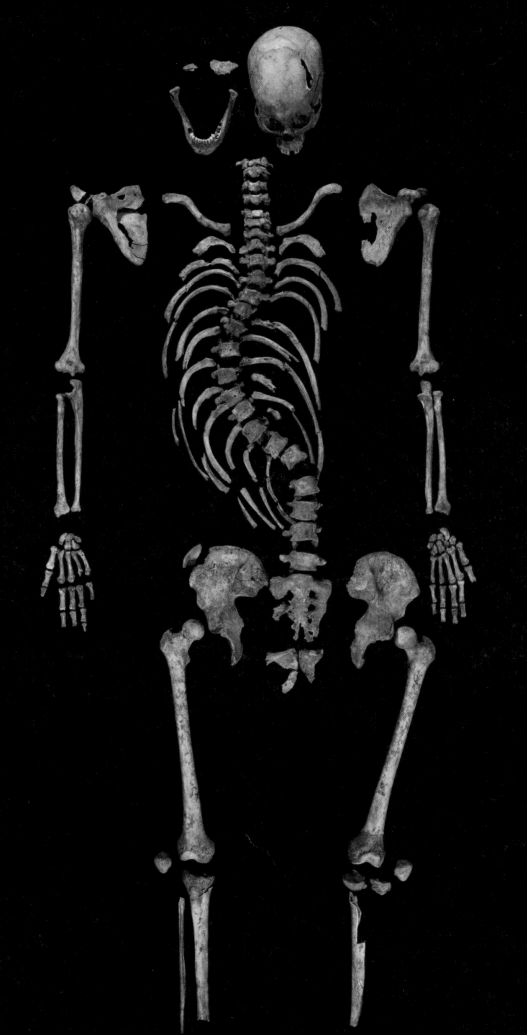

Philippa couldn't believe it! It wasn't certain proof that it was Richard III, but so far, this was great evidence. News got out that skeletal remains had been found under the parking lot. People from everywhere came to see the dig. Over the next few days, the team worked to uncover the fragile bones. Once removed, they were taken to a laboratory for study. In order to prove that these were really the long lost remains of King Richard III, many tests needed to be done. What no one could expect, however, was just how *much* the tests would reveal.

An actor portrays Richard III.

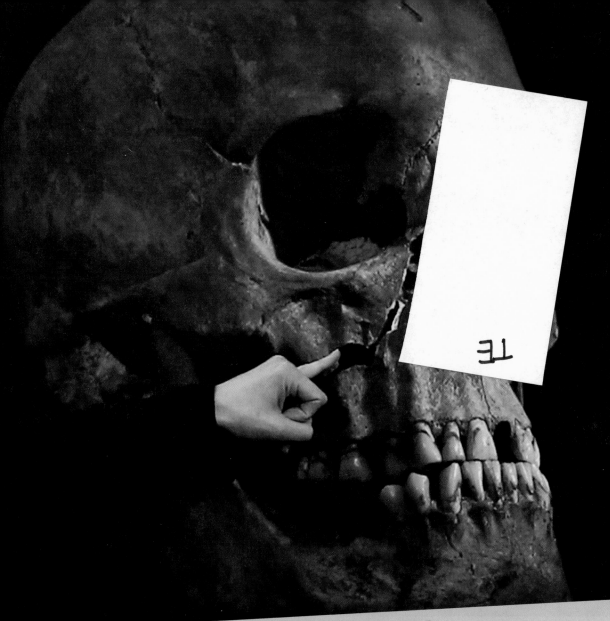

31

IF BONES COULD SPEAK

From the moment the skeleton was found, it began providing clues about the man it belonged to. First, scientists can tell how old a skeleton is by using a test called carbon dating. The carbon dating revealed that the person must have died between 1455 and 1540. King Richard III died in 1485. A match!

Secondly, closer study of the curved spine showed them that the man didn't actually have a hunched back—he had suffered from scoliosis, a condition that causes a curved spine. One shoulder might lift higher than the other, making the person appear hunchbacked. Together with reports that Richard III was a hunchback, this was even more amazing evidence.

Next was the skull. There was much damage to it. A large hole in the back clearly had clean cuts around the edges, suggesting that the man had been hit in the head with a very sharp object. They found eight blows to the head, including a small, rectangular hole in the cheek caused by a dagger. Since Richard III died in battle, this would make sense. This also meant something else—either he lost his helmet in battle or he rode onto the battlefield wearing his crown instead, making him an easy target.

Another interesting fact was that his arm bones were slightly thinner than average for a man. Because some historical records say that the king was an excellent fighter despite his thin frame, this made the case even stronger. The skeleton also helped to put the rumor to rest that one of the king's arms was shorter than the other, a monstrous depiction, thanks to Shakespeare's play.

Probably the best piece of evidence, though, came with the help of genealogists, who study families, and forensic scientists, who use DNA to, among other things, match people to their ancestors. (DNA is a code of cells which makes up all living things.) Richard III's ancestors were traced back over 17 generations to two descendants alive today in Canada. Scientists were able to match cell samples taken from the skeleton with cell samples from the two family members. The two DNA strands matched. That proved it—the skeleton found was that of King Richard III of England!

Once the king's identity was confirmed, one last specialist was called in. Caroline Wilkinson, an expert in facial reconstruction, uses computers to recreate what a dead person might have looked like when they were alive. After measuring the size and shape of the skull, eye sockets, jaw line, and cheekbones, Caroline was able to get a good idea of King Richard III's appearance. Using this information, she was able to use computer technology to reconstruct his face. Everyone was astonished to find that he looked very similar to the paintings created of him with one exception—he would have appeared younger and kinder, not old and mean as the artists made him seem.

Portrait of Richard III

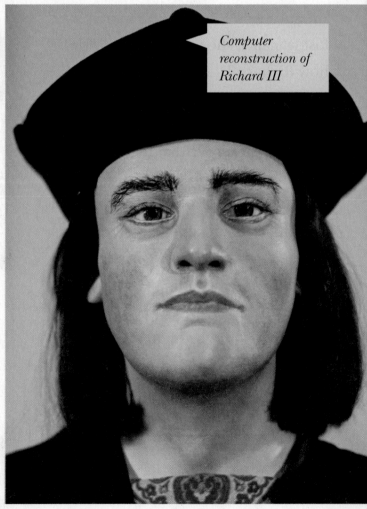

Computer reconstruction of Richard III

Soon afterwards, Philippa and her team ordered a model of the king's head to be made for everyone to see. This will be on display at the Yorkshire Museum in England. There, visitors can gaze upon his face and wonder if the king was as youthful and handsome as his skull seemed to suggest, or if he indeed appeared as a deformed tyrant. Once all tests are over, the king's remains will be buried in a new location where he can be properly remembered.

Philippa Langley could not be more pleased. She began her search with nothing but a dream and a slim chance of succeeding. But not only did she succeed in finding the monarch's lost remains, she was also able to show how Richard III may not have been the horrible monster his successors made him out to be.

Does this prove that the 500-year-old king was not an evil tyrant? Not really. The truth is—we will never know. But thanks to archaeologists, scientists, and historical reports, we now have a clearer understanding of who King Richard III really was. So, the next time you are walking through a parking lot, stop, look down, and close your eyes. You never know what mysteries may lie beneath your feet, waiting to be discovered.

SPIDER

by Shel Silverstein

A spider lives inside my head
Who weaves a strange and wondrous web
Of silken threads and silver strings
To catch all sorts of flying things,
Like crumbs of thoughts and bits of smiles
And specks of dried-up tears,
And dust of dreams that catch and cling
For years and years and years. . . .

THE FROG

by Hilaire Belloc

Be kind and tender to the Frog,
    And do not call him names,
As "Slimy-skin," or "Polly-wog,"
    Or likewise "Ugly James,"
Or "Gap-a-grin," or "Toad-gone-wrong,"
    Or "Bill Bandy-knees":
The Frog is justly sensitive
    To epithets like these.
No animal will more repay
    A treatment kind and fair;
At least so lonely people say
Who keep a frog (and, by the way,
They are extremely rare).

Go Southward, Birds!

by Elizabeth Coatsworth

Clap hands! clap wings!
go southward, birds!
The winter's near
with snow like curds,
and frost whose touch
is strange and light–
seek your hot suns
with wings and flight!

Clap hands! clap wings!
why linger here?
The snow will drift,
the winds blow drear.
Go! robin, bluebird,
wren and swallow!
Fly! fly ahead!
and we will follow!

THE JELLYFISH AND THE CLAM

by Jeff Moss

Said the clam to the pink jellyfish,
"You're no more than a lump of wet squish!
You've no backbone or brain,
You're too dull to explain,
When they look at you, people go 'Ish'"

Said the jellyfish back to the clam,
"I may look like thin raspberry jam,
But you're just a thick shell
And you don't even jell,
So I'm happy to be what I am!"

Well, I say let's give three big cheers
For these two and their lengthy careers.
Though they both may be dull,
With no spine and no skull,
Still they've lasted a half-billion years!

skeletons

by Valerie Worth

Is it the
Curve of their
Breezy ribs, the
Crook of their
Elegant fingers,

Their eyeless
Eyes, so wide
And wise,
Their silent
Ivory laughter,

The frisk and
Prance of their
Skittering dance
With never a
Pause for breath,

That fill us
With such
Delicious delight,
While scaring us
Half to death?

To the Skeleton of a Dinosaur in the Museum

by Lilian Moore

Hey there, Brontosaurus!
You were here so long before us
Your deeds can never bore us.
How were the good old days?

Did you really like to graze?
Did you often munch
With a prehistoric crunch
On a giant tree—or two—or three
For lunch?

As you went yon and hither
Were you ever in a dither
When your head and distant tail
Went different ways?

Did you shake the earth like thunder
With your roars and groans?
I wonder. . . . Say it's hard
To have a conversation
With your bones.

50

from *AMERICAN TALL TALES*
by Mary Pope Osborne
Wood engravings by Michael McCurdy

PECOS BILL

NOTES ON THE STORY

YARNS ABOUT PECOS BILL, "the greatest cowpuncher ever known on
either side of the Rockies, from Texas through Montana and on
into Canada," first appeared in a 1923 *Century Magazine*. The
author of the piece, Edward O'Reilly, wrote the "saga" of Pecos
Bill by combining a number of western folklore episodes with
the boastful, comic tall-tale language of heroes such as Davy
Crockett and Paul Bunyan.

After O'Reilly invented the character of Pecos Bill, many
others revised and expanded upon the yarns in dozens of books,
articles, poems, recordings, and plays. Pecos Bill seemed to
capture the spirit of an earlier America—wild, untamed, and
unsocialized. He even added an occasional note of his own brand
of recklessness to stories about other tall-tale characters as well.
In an original Febold Feboldson story, Febold and Pecos Bill have
a shoot-out. And in a Paul Bunyan anthology, Pecos Bill teaches
Paul how to ride a streak of lightning. This tale about Pecos
Bill was derived from the O'Reilly saga as well as a number of
other retellings.

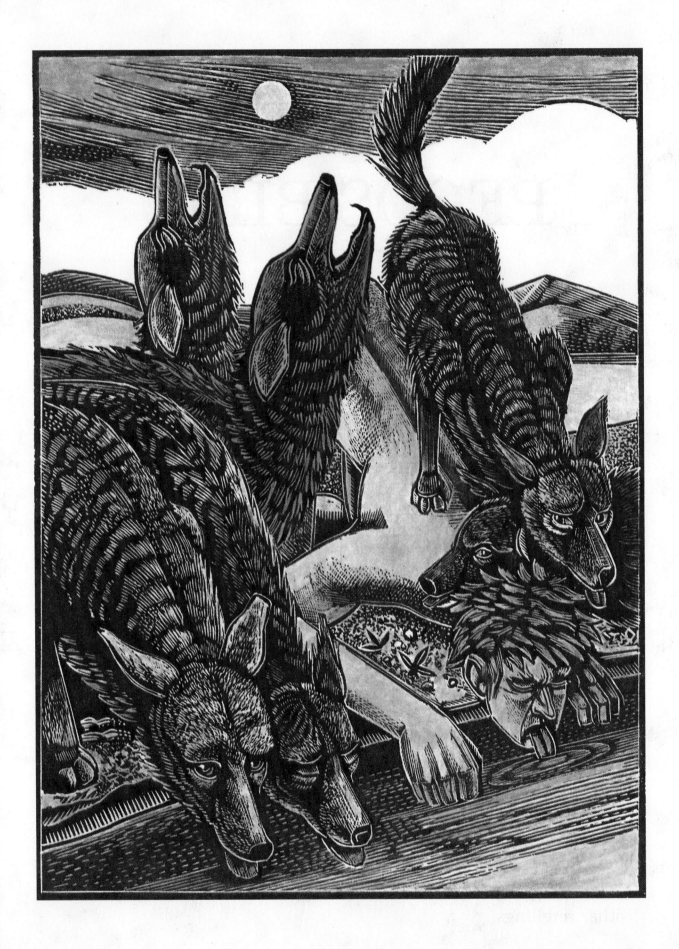

Ask any coyote near the Pecos River in western Texas who was the best cowboy who ever lived, and he'll throw back his head and howl, "Ah-hooo!" If you didn't know already, that's coyote language for *Pecos Bill*.

When Pecos Bill was a little baby, he was as tough as a pine knot. He teethed on horseshoes instead of teething rings and played with grizzly bears instead of teddy bears. He could have grown up just fine in the untamed land of eastern Texas. But one day his pappy ran in from the fields, hollering, "Pack up, Ma! Neighbors movin' in fifty miles away! It's gettin' too crowded!"

Before sundown Bill's folks loaded their fifteen kids and all their belongings into their covered wagon and started west.

As they clattered across the desolate land of western Texas, the crushing heat nearly drove them all crazy. Baby Bill got so hot and cross that he began to wallop his big brothers. Pretty soon all fifteen kids were going at one another tooth and nail. Before they turned each other into catfish bait, Bill fell out of the wagon and landed *kerplop* on the sun-scorched desert.

The others were so busy fighting that they didn't even notice the baby was missing until it was too late to do anything about it.

Well, tough little Bill just sat there in the dirt, watching his family rattle off in a cloud of dust, until an old coyote walked over and sniffed him.

"Goo-goo!" Bill said.

Now it's an amazing coincidence, but "Goo-goo" happens to mean something similar to "Glad to meet you" in coyote language. Naturally the old coyote figured he'd come across one of his own kind. He gave Bill a big lick and picked him up by the scruff of the neck and carried him home to his den.

Bill soon discovered the coyote's kinfolk were about the wildest, roughest bunch you could imagine. Before he knew it, he was roaming the prairies with the pack. He howled at the moon, sniffed the brush, and chased lizards across the sand. He was having such a good time, scuttling about naked and dirty on all fours, that he completely forgot what it was like to be a human.

Pecos Bill's coyote days came to an end about seventeen years later. One evening as he was sniffing the sagebrush, a cowpoke came loping by on a big horse. "Hey, you!" he shouted. "What in the world are you?"

Bill sat on his haunches and stared at the feller.

"What *are* you?" asked the cowpoke again.

"Varmint," said Bill hoarsely, for he hadn't used his human voice in seventeen years.

"No, you ain't!"

"Yeah, I am. I got fleas, don't I?"

"Well, that don't mean nothing. A lot of Texans got fleas. The thing varmints got that you ain't got is a tail."

"Oh, yes, I do have a tail," said Pecos Bill.

"Lemme see it then," said the cowpoke.

Bill turned around to look at his rear end, and for the first time in his life he realized he didn't have a tail.

"Dang," he said. "But if I'm not a varmint, what am I?"

"You're a cowboy! So start acting like one!"

Bill just growled at the feller like any coyote worth his salt would. But deep down in his heart of hearts he knew the cowpoke was right. For the last seventeen years he'd had a sneaking suspicion that he was different from that pack of coyotes. For one thing, none of them seemed to smell quite as bad as he did.

So with a heavy heart he said good-bye to his four-legged friends and took off with the cowpoke for the nearest ranch.

Acting like a human wasn't all that easy for Pecos Bill. Even though he soon started dressing right, he never bothered to shave or comb his hair. He'd just throw some water on his face in the morning and go around the rest of the day looking like a wet dog. Ignorant cowpokes claimed Bill wasn't too smart. Some of the meaner ones liked to joke that he wore a ten-dollar hat on a five-cent head.

The truth was Pecos Bill would soon prove to be one of the greatest cowboys who ever lived. He just needed to find the kind of folks who'd appreciate him. One night when he was licking his dinner plate, his ears perked up. A couple of ranch hands were going on about a gang of wild cowboys.

"Yep. Those fellas are more animal than human," one ranch hand was saying.

"Yep. Them's the toughest bunch I ever come across. Heck, they're so tough, they can kick fire out of flint rock with their bare toes!"

"Yep. 'N' they like to bite nails in half for fun!"

"Who are these fellers?" asked Bill.

"The Hell's Gate Gang," said the ranch hand. "The mangiest, meanest, most low-down bunch of low-life varmints that ever grew hair."

"Sounds like my kind of folks," said Bill, and before anyone could holler whoa, he jumped on his horse and took off for Hell's Gate Canyon.

Bill hadn't gone far when disaster struck. His horse stepped in a hole and broke its ankle.

"Dang!" said Bill as he stumbled up from the spill. He draped the lame critter around his neck and hurried on.

After he'd walked about a hundred more miles, Bill heard some mean rattling. Then a fifty-foot rattlesnake reared up its ugly head and stuck out its long, forked tongue, ready to fight.

"Knock it off, you scaly-hided fool. I'm in a hurry," Bill said.

The snake didn't give a spit for Bill's plans. He just rattled on.

Before the cussed varmint could strike, Bill had no choice but to knock him cross-eyed. "Hey, feller," he said, holding up the dazed snake. "I like your spunk. Come go with us." Then he wrapped the rattler around his arm and continued on his way.

After Bill had hiked another hundred miles with his horse around his neck and his snake around his arm, he heard a terrible growl. A huge mountain lion was crouching on a cliff, getting ready to leap on top of him.

"Don't jump, you mangy bobtailed fleabag!" Bill said.

Well, call any mountain lion a mangy bobtailed fleabag, and he'll jump on your back for sure. After this one leaped onto Bill, so much fur began to fly that it darkened the sky. Bill wrestled that mountain lion into a headlock, then squeezed him so tight that the big cat had to cry uncle.

When the embarrassed old critter started to slink off, Bill felt sorry for him. "Aw, c'mon, you big silly," he said. "You're more like me than most humans I meet."

He saddled up the cat, jumped on his back, and the four of them headed for the canyon, with the mountain lion screeching, the horse neighing, the rattler rattling, and Pecos Bill hollering a wild war whoop.

When the Hell's Gate Gang heard those noises coming from the prairie, they nearly fainted. They dropped their dinner plates, and their faces turned as white as bleached desert bones. Their knees knocked and their six-guns shook.

"Hey, there!" Bill said as he sidled up to their campfire, grinning. "Who's the boss around here?"

A nine-foot feller with ten pistols at his sides stepped forward and in a shaky voice said, "Stranger, I was. But from now on, it'll be you."

"Well, thanky, pardner," said Bill. "Get on with your dinner, boys. Don't let me interrupt."

Once Bill settled down with the Hell's Gate Gang, his true genius revealed itself. With his gang's help, he put together the biggest ranch in the southwest. He used New Mexico as a corral and Arizona as a pasture. He invented tarantulas and scorpions as practical jokes. He also invented roping. Some say his rope was exactly as long as the equator; others argue it was two feet shorter.

Things were going fine for Bill until Texas began to suffer the worst drought in its history. It was so dry that all the rivers turned as powdery as biscuit flour. The parched grass was catching fire everywhere. For a while Bill and his gang managed to lasso water from the Rio Grande. When that river dried up, they lassoed water from the Gulf of Mexico.

No matter what he did, though, Bill couldn't get enough water to stay ahead of the drought. All his horses and cows were starting to dry up and blow away like balls of tumbleweed. It was horrible.

Just when the end seemed near, the sky turned a deep shade of purple. From the distant mountains came a terrible roar. The cattle began to stampede, and a huge black funnel of a cyclone appeared, heading straight for Bill's ranch.

The rest of the Hell's Gate Gang shouted, "Help!" and ran.

But Pecos Bill wasn't scared in the least. "Yahoo!" he hollered, and he swung his lariat and lassoed that cyclone around its neck.

Bill held on tight as he got sucked up into the middle of the swirling cloud. He grabbed the cyclone by the ears and pulled himself onto her back. Then he let out a whoop and headed that twister across Texas.

The mighty cyclone bucked, arched, and screamed like a wild bronco. But Pecos Bill just held on with his legs and used his strong hands to wring the rain out of her wind. He wrung out rain that flooded Texas, New Mexico, and Arizona, until finally he slid off the shriveled-up funnel and fell into California. The earth sank about two hundred feet below sea level in the spot where Bill landed, creating the area known today as Death Valley.

"There. That little waterin' should hold things for a while," he said, brushing himself off.

After his cyclone ride, no horse was too wild for Pecos Bill. He soon found a young colt that was as tough as a tiger and as crazy as a streak of lightning. He named the colt Widow Maker and raised him on barbed wire and dynamite. Whenever the two rode together, they back-flipped and somersaulted all over Texas, loving every minute of it.

One day when Bill and Widow Maker were bouncing around
the Pecos River, they came across an awesome sight: a wild-
looking, red-haired woman riding on the back of the biggest catfish
Bill had ever seen. The woman looked like she was having a ball,
screeching, "Ride 'em, cowgirl!" as the catfish whipped her around
in the air.

"What's your name?" Bill shouted.

"Slue-foot Sue! What's it to you?" she said. Then she war-
whooped away over the windy water.

Thereafter all Pecos Bill could think of was Slue-foot Sue. He
spent more and more time away from the Hell's Gate Gang as he
wandered the barren cattle-lands, looking for her. When he finally
found her lonely little cabin, he was so love-struck he reverted
to some of his old coyote ways. He sat on his haunches in the
moonlight and began a-howling and ah-hooing.

Well, the good news was that Sue had a bit of coyote in her too, so she completely understood Bill's language. She stuck her head out her window and ah-hooed back to him that she loved him, too. Consequently Bill and Sue decided to get married.

On the day of the wedding Sue wore a beautiful white dress with steel-spring bustle, and Bill appeared in an elegant buckskin suit.

But after a lovely ceremony, a terrible catastrophe occurred. Slue-foot Sue got it into her head that she just had to have a ride on Bill's wild bronco, Widow Maker.

"You can't do that, honey," Bill said. "He won't let any human toss a leg over him but me."

"Don't worry," said Sue. "You know I can ride anything on four legs, not to mention what flies or swims."

Bill tried his best to talk Sue out of it, but she wouldn't listen. She was dying to buck on the back of that bronco. Wearing her white wedding dress with the bustle, she jumped on Widow Maker and kicked him with her spurs.

Well, that bronco didn't need any thorns in his side to start bucking to beat the band. He bounded up in the air with such amazing force that suddenly Sue was flying high into the Texas sky. She flew over plains and mesas, over canyons, deserts, and prairies. She flew so high that she looped over the new moon and fell back to earth.

But when Sue landed on her steel-spring bustle, she rebounded right back into the heavens! As she bounced back and forth, between heaven and earth, Bill whirled his lariat above his head, then lassoed her. But instead of bringing Sue back down to earth, he got yanked into the night sky alongside her!

Together Pecos Bill and Slue-foot Sue bounced off the earth and went flying to the moon. And at that point Bill must have gotten some sort of foothold in a moon crater--because neither he nor Sue returned to earth. Not ever.

Folks figure those two must have dug their boot heels into some moon cheese and raised a pack of wild coyotes just like themselves. Texans'll tell you that every time you hear thunder rolling over the desolate land near the Pecos River, it's just Bill's family having a good laugh upstairs. When you hear a strange ah-hooing in the dark night, don't be fooled---that's the sound of Bill howling *on* the moon instead of *at* it. And when lights flash across the midnight sky, you can bet it's Bill and Sue riding the backs of some white-hot shooting stars.

from *AMERICAN TALL TALES*
by Mary Pope Osborne
Wood engravings by Michael McCurdy

JOHN HENRY

NOTES ON THE STORY

AFTER THE CIVIL WAR, the Chesapeake & Ohio Railroad Company laid hundreds of miles of railroad track through West Virginia. These new railroad routes opened up timber and coal lands and created new towns. When the tracks reached the Alleghenies, the railroad company hired more than a thousand laborers to build tunnels through the mountains. The tunnels were created by blasting through the mountain shale. This work was done by "steel drivers," men who drilled steel spikes into the solid rock. Once the holes were drilled, they were packed with dynamite. Since the early West Virginia tunnels had no safety regulations, these tunnel workers were exposed to an early death from the dynamite explosions, falling rock, and lethal dust created by the blasts.

Starting in the 1870s, a black steel driver named John Henry became the subject of many of the work songs sung by railroad-tunnel gangs. Like most work songs, the John Henry songs consisted of a few short lines repeated several times with pauses in between for the stroke of a pick or hammer. Historians disagree about whether John Henry was based on a real man or not. Some believe that he can be traced to John Hardy, a true-life subject of popular ballads who was also a superior steel driver; others believe that a man named John Henry actually worked on the Big Bend tunnel in the Alleghenies.

Whether John Henry was real or mythical, he was a strong, enduring character to many southern black laborers. Later, when songs about him were recorded and played on the radio, he became known to the general public as well.

The night John Henry was born the sky was as black as coal, thunder rolled through the heavens, and the earth trembled.

"This boy is special," the preacher said as folks gathered in the cabin by the river to see the new baby.

In the dim lantern light, John Henry was the most powerful-looking baby folks had ever seen. His arms were as thick as stovepipes. He had great broad shoulders and strong muscles. And as folks stared at him, he opened his eyes and smiled a smile that lit up the southern night.

When John Henry raised his arm, folks gasped and brought their hands to their faces, for they saw that the mighty baby had been born with a hammer in his hand. Then they all began to laugh and felt happier than they had in a long, long time.

John Henry grew up fast in a world that didn't let children stay children for long. Before he was six, he was carrying stones for the railroad gangs that were building tracks through the land of West Virginia.

By the time he was ten, he was hammering steel from dawn till dark. No train whistle in America sang as loud as John Henry's mighty hammer. It rang like silver and shone like gold. It flashed up through the air, making a wide arc more than nineteen feet, then crashed down, driving a steel spike six inches into solid rock.

By the time he was a young man, John Henry was the best steel driver in the whole country. He could hammer for hours without missing a beat, so fast that his hammer moved like lightning. He had to keep a pail of water nearby to cool it down, and he wore out two handles a day. All the railroad bosses wanted John Henry to work for them. When the Chesapeake and Ohio started making a tunnel in the Allegheny Mountains, they asked him to lead their force of steel-driving men.

Soon John Henry was whistling and singing in the early summer light as he walked to work in the mountain tunnel. Beside him was his wife, Lucy, with eyes as bright as stars and hair as wavy as the sea. Lucy was a steel driver herself. At noontime she drove the spikes while John Henry sat with their little boy, Johnny, in the sunny mountain grass and ate his lunch of ham hocks and biscuits with molasses.

Lifting Johnny high into the air, John Henry shouted, "Someday you're going to be a steel-driving man like your daddy!"

July of that summer was the hottest month on record in West Virginia. Working in the terrible heat, many of the steel drivers collapsed by noon. But John Henry tried to protect their jobs by picking up their hammers and doing their work too. One week he did his own work and the work of four others as well. He hammered day and night, barely stopping for meals.

When the men tried to thank John Henry, he just smiled and said, "A man ain't nothing but a man. He's just got to do his best."

August was hotter than July. One day as the men labored in the white light of the afternoon sun, a city salesman drove up to the work site. "Come see, everybody!" he shouted. "Lookee here at this incredible invention! A steam drill that can drill holes faster than a dozen men working together!"

"Aw, I don't know about that," said the railroad boss, rubbing his grizzly jaw. "I got the best steel driver in the country. His name is John Henry, and he can beat *two* dozen men working together."

"That's impossible," the salesman said. "But if you can prove your hand driller is faster than my steam driller, I'll give you this machine for free."

The boss called to John Henry, "This fellow doubts which of you can drill faster. How about a big contest?"

As John Henry stared at the steam drill, he saw a picture of the future. He saw machines taking over the jobs of the country's finest workers. He saw himself and his friends out of work and begging beside the road. He saw men robbed of their dignity and robbed of their families.

"I'd rather die with my hammer in my hand than let that steam drill run me down," he yelled back. And his boss and friends all cheered.

"That contest will be the death of you, John Henry," Lucy said later. "You got a wife and child, and if anything happens to you, we won't ever smile again."

John Henry just lifted Johnny into the air and said, "Honey, a man ain't nothing but a man. But a man's always got to do his best. And tomorrow I'm going to take my hammer and drive that steel faster than any machine!"

Lucy put on her best blue dress, and folks came from all over Ohio, Virginia, and Kentucky. They came from the countryside, and they came from the cities.

At half past six in the morning, John Henry and the salesman with the steam-powered drill stood side by side. Early as it was, the sun was burning hot. There was no breeze. Sweat poured down people's faces like water down a hill.

As the onlookers gathered around the contestants, Little Bill, the worker who loved John Henry the best, said, "There ain't a steam drill anywheres that can beat that man!"

But the city folks, who had staked their hopes on the future of machines, said, "He won't beat that drill unless the rocks in the mountain turn to gold!"

"No, sirree!" said Jimmy, John Henry's oldest friend. "Before that drill wins, he'll make the mountain fall!"

Bang!----the race was on! As the steam-drill salesman turned on the steam, John Henry kissed the smooth handle of his hammer.

At first the steam drill drove the steel twice as fast as John Henry did. But then he grabbed another hammer and started working with a hammer in each hand. He went faster and faster, striking blow after blow as he tunneled into the mountain.

"That man's a mighty man," a city man shouted, "but he'll weaken when the hardest rock is found."

"Not John Henry! Just listen to that steel ring!" Little Bill said.

"I believe these mountains are caving in!" said the city man.

"No, they're not. That's his hammers you hear in the wind," Jimmy cried.

Inside the dark tunnel, where the yellow dust and heat were so thick that most men would have smothered, John Henry hammered faster and faster. As clouds of stone dust billowed from the mouth of the tunnel, the crowd shouted and screamed. John Henry's hammers sounded like ten thousand hammers.

Lucy, Little Bill, and Jimmy cheered when the steam drill was dragged out of the tunnel. Sputtering and spewing, it had broken down.

"Come back now, John Henry!" Lucy shouted.

But John Henry kept hammering, hammering faster than any man had ever hammered before, hammering against all the machines of the future. As his hammer glowed white-hot, he tunneled deeper into the darkness, driving the steel so hard that the mighty ribs of his body began to crack, and his insides broke in two, and his great heart burst.

When John Henry fell, it sounded like an earthquake.

There was a terrible silence inside the mountain. Lucy stood still as stone, for she knew what had happened.

When Jimmy and Little Bill brought him out of the tunnel, John Henry's blood ran red over the ground. But his hands still clutched one of his mighty hammers. "I've beat them," he gasped. "Now I'm dying."

"Don't go, John Henry!" Lucy begged.

"Bring me a cool drink of water, honey," he said. Then he took his last breath.

Lucy fell down on her knees and sobbed. "Lord, this was a good man," she said.

They carried John Henry down from the mountain. They carried him to the river and buried him in the sand near the cabin where he was born.

Folks stood in the rain and flagged the westbound train headed for John Henry's grave. And word spread quickly across the land: "John Henry's never coming back."

Soon the steam drill and other new machines took over the work of the steel-driving men. Little Bill, Jimmy, and others like them left their families and wandered north and west, looking for work. As they walked the hot, dusty roads, they took the only jobs they could find. They picked cotton and dug ditches. But often while they worked, they sang about John Henry:

John Henry told his friends,
"A man ain't nothing but a man.
Before I'll be beat by that big steam drill,
I'll die with my hammer in my hand,
I'll die with my hammer in my hand."

How the Stars Fell into the Sky
A Navajo Legend

by Jerrie Oughton
Illustrated by Lisa Desimini

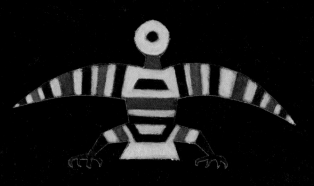

This is a retelling of a legend told
to the Navajo Indians by Hosteen Klah,
their great medicine man,
at the turn of the twentieth century.
It is part of the mythology that details the
mysteries of Earth in the beginning.

When the pulse of the first day carried it to the rim of night, First Woman said to First Man, "The people need to know the laws. To help them, we must write the laws for all to see."

"Write them in the sand," he told her.

"But the wind will blow them away," she answered.

"Write them on the water then," he said and turned to go, having more important matters on his mind.

"But they will disappear the moment I write them on the water," First Woman called out.

First Man turned back impatiently and looked at her squatting there
on the rim of the night, a blanket of stars at her feet.

"Why don't you write them in the sky?" he said.

"Take your jewels there and write them in the sky."

And so she began, slowly, first one and then the next, placing her jewels across the dome of night, carefully designing her pattern so all could read it.

But First Woman was not alone. Behind a low
tree Coyote crouched, watching her as she crafted
her careful mosaic on the blackberry cloth of night.
He crept closer.

"What are you doing?" he called to her in a voice that sounded like
the whine of an arrow whistling in the wind. "Why are you tacking
up the night sky with your jewels?"

"Oh," she answered, deliberately shifting a star, "I am writing the laws so all the people can read them. There will be no confusion if we can always see the laws."

Her hands glowed from the warmth of the stars she
was touching, and she smiled as she toiled.
"May I help?" Coyote asked.
First Woman nodded. "Begin here," she said and
handed him a star.

Coyote hung the star and stepped back to look.
He hung another, and another. But for each star he
hung, First Woman's blanket held a hundred
thousand more.

"This is slow work," he grumbled.

"Writing the laws could take many moons," she said
and began humming to herself.

"Can't we find a faster way and be done?"
Coyote asked.

"Why finish?" she answered. "What is there to
do next that is half so important as writing the laws?"

"The people will see these laws before they enter their hogans at night."

"The young mother will sing of them to her child."

"The lonely warrior, crouching in an unknown country, will look up and warm himself by them."

"Writing the laws may be what I do each night for the rest of my life."
But Coyote lacked First Woman's patience. He loved best to see a job finished.

Impatiently he gathered two corners of First Woman's blanket, and
before she could stop him . . .

. . . he flung the remaining stars out into the night, spilling them in wild disarray, shattering First Woman's careful patterns.

First Woman leaned far into the night and watched the tumbling stars. "What have you done, you foolish animal!" she shrieked at Coyote. He crept away while First Woman wept because there was no undoing what Coyote had done.

As the pulse of the second day brought it into being, the people rose and went about their lives, never knowing in what foolish haste Coyote had tumbled the stars . . .

. . . never knowing the reason for the confusion that would always dwell among them.

Northwest Coast Peoples

by Lois Markham

Land of Salmon and Cedars

Thousands of years ago, humans began to settle along the narrow strip of land that hugs the Pacific Coast from what is now southern Alaska to southern Oregon. It was a land of abundance. Fish and sea mammals crowded the ocean. In spring, salmon left their ocean homes to swim up streams, where they were easily caught. The nearby forests provided berries, meat, and edible roots. The mild, rainy climate resulted in thick forests of evergreen trees, particularly cedars, which the people used to make shelter, clothing, and transportation.

The social practices of the region differed from those of other Native American groups in three major ways. First, it was the only culture in the Americas not influenced by the Maya and Aztec cultures of Central America. Second, the people developed an advanced lifestyle without practicing agriculture or making pottery. Third, since food was easily available, the people had time to spend on producing material goods. Thus, the people of the Northwest Coast were one of the few Native American groups to place importance on acquiring possessions.

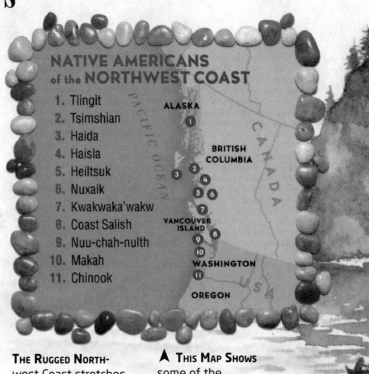

NATIVE AMERICANS of the NORTHWEST COAST

1. Tlingit
2. Tsimshian
3. Haida
4. Haisla
5. Heiltsuk
6. Nuxalk
7. Kwakwaka'wakw
8. Coast Salish
9. Nuu-chah-nulth
10. Makah
11. Chinook

THE RUGGED NORTH- west Coast stretches 2,000 miles from north to south, but it is only 100 to 150 miles wide. Mountains separate it from the rest of the continent. Offshore are many islands, which are the tips of submerged mountains.

▲ **THIS MAP SHOWS** some of the major groups of Native Americans who lived along the Northwest Coast. The groups spoke different languages and had unique variations in lifestyles that distingushed them. They were further divided into tribes, clans, and family groups.

TALL CARVED POLES made from cedar logs decorated many villages and homes. The figures carved on the poles represented the totems (animals or mythological creatures) from which a family traced its origins.

THE NATIVE Americans of the Northwest Coast traveled almost everywhere by canoe. Formed from hollowed-out cedar logs, canoes were made in different sizes and shapes for different uses. Larger canoes might be used for carrying trade goods, traveling to ceremonies, or raiding other villages. Individual families had smaller general-use canoes.

IN LATE SPRING, salmon leave the ocean to swim up freshwater streams where they lay their eggs. There were so many salmon that it was easy to catch them with a dip net or spear. Sometimes, Northwest Coast peoples built wooden dams, called weirs, to trap the fish so they could be caught even more easily.

105

Village Life

The villages of Northwest Coast peoples were built on a beach, often where a river or stream flowed into the ocean. A river gave villagers easy access to the inland. A village consisted of one or more rows of wooden houses facing the ocean. Here, the people lived in the fall and winter months. In the spring and summer, however, they moved to temporary dwellings further inland. There, they hunted and gathered berries and roots to be dried and eaten in the winter. Since they collected enough food in spring and summer to last through the winter, their winter months were spent creating art, telling stories, and feasting at elaborate ceremonies.

▲ VILLAGE HOUSES WERE made of cedar. A rectangular frame was constructed of logs. The walls were made of planks, so the houses are called plank houses, or sometimes long houses or big houses. The planks were leaned against the frame or tied to it with woven cedar rope. The planks could be easily removed and brought to a family's temporary summer camp, where they were attached to a frame left standing there. The outside of a plank house might be painted with symbols representing the family's heritage. Totem poles might be part of the frame or stand alone in front of a house. This picture shows a Haida village in 1878.

▲ **IN THE SOUTHERN** part of the region, people covered the frames of their summer huts with mats woven from reeds or cedar bark rather than planks.

▲ **VILLAGERS WOULD** gratefully kill a whale that had been stranded in shallow water and use every part of its body. But only the Nuu-chah-nulth and Makah hunted whales in the open ocean. Whale hunting was dangerous. Eight men would follow

and kill a 50-foot whale using only harpoons made of mussel shells and ropes made from spruce roots. The success of the hunt depended on the chief harpooner, who would have been chosen by a special spirit as a boy and received years of training.

was the most important food. It was eaten fresh in spring and summer. The excess catch was dried. In winter, dried fish was boiled, steamed, or baked. Fish oil, rich in nutrients, was used as an all-purpose sauce. A favorite winter treat was dried berries in fish oil.

▲ **BERRIES, ROOTS,** shellfish, and meat were eaten fresh or dried in winter. Fish

▲ **SOME GROUPS** were more war-like than others. Warriors wore wooden armor, including helmets that were carved and painted to make a warrior look larger

and fiercer. Surprise nighttime attacks of neighboring villages were often made in war canoes. The aim was to capture enemies, who then became the slaves of their captors.

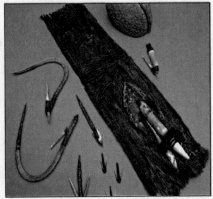

▲ **IN THE EARLY** 1700s, a sudden mudslide buried the Makah village of Ozette. The mud preserved the village much as it was. Between 1970 and 1981, the site was excavated, bringing

to light carved house boards; baskets; wooden boxes; clothing; cradle boards; mats; hats; looms; toys; equipment for whaling, fishing, and sealing; tools; and ceremonial gear.

▲ **THE PEOPLE OF THE** Northwest traded all along the coast. Some groups even traded with inland peoples for raw materials they did not have. Traded goods included dried foods,

sea otter skins, carved wooden dishes, canoes, baskets, and blankets. Rare dentalia shells (above), found off the coast of Vancouver Island, were sometimes used as a kind of money.

➤ **SUMMERS WERE** so mild that little clothing was needed. Skirts and capes made from the soft inner bark of the cedar tree were used as protection from the rain. Winter clothing was made from watertight deerskin. Hats were used for protection from rain and sun and also for ceremonial purposes. They were woven

from grasses or carved from wood and often painted with animal designs.

Family Life

People of the Northwest Coast often lived in villages that were divided into two groups, called moieties (MOY-uh-tees). Each moiety was composed of clans. A village might include two to several clans. The members of a clan considered themselves related because they shared the same spirit ancestor. Clans were part of larger groups called phratries (FRAY-trees). Their primary purpose was to govern marriage rules and provide aid. People from the same clan, moiety, or phratry could not marry.

Each clan had three ranks of people: nobles, commoners, and slaves. Nobles were the richest members of their clan. Commoners were respected members of a clan, but they had less wealth than nobles. Families could gain or lose social status by increasing or losing their wealth. Slaves were captives from other villages. They could not change their status. Usually, several related families lived together in a plank house, which was owned by the wealthiest man.

IT WAS DARK INSIDE a plank house because there were no windows. A small oily fish called eulachon could be used for light. When a cedar wick was pulled through the fish, it burned like a candle. The fish came to be called candlefish.

A POPULAR GAME WAS hoop and pole, in which rivals tried to toss pointed sticks through a ring that was rolled along the ground. A ball game called shinny was similar to field hockey. Wrestling, arm wrestling, and finger wrestling were also popular.

WOVEN MATS or wooden screens were used to divide the living space and give each family some privacy.

CLOTHES, FOOD, AND tools were stored in wooden boxes or baskets.

BABIES WERE BATHED daily, rubbed with whale oil, dusted with willow ash powder, and wrapped in cedar-bark diapers. They spent the first year of life in a cradleboard, which a mother could strap to her back or lean against a tree while she worked. Since a flat head was considered beautiful and a mark of status, noble and commoner babies had their heads flattened. A board was placed over the forehead and attached to both sides of the cradleboard for the first few months of a baby's life. It was not painful. The children of slaves did not have their heads flattened.

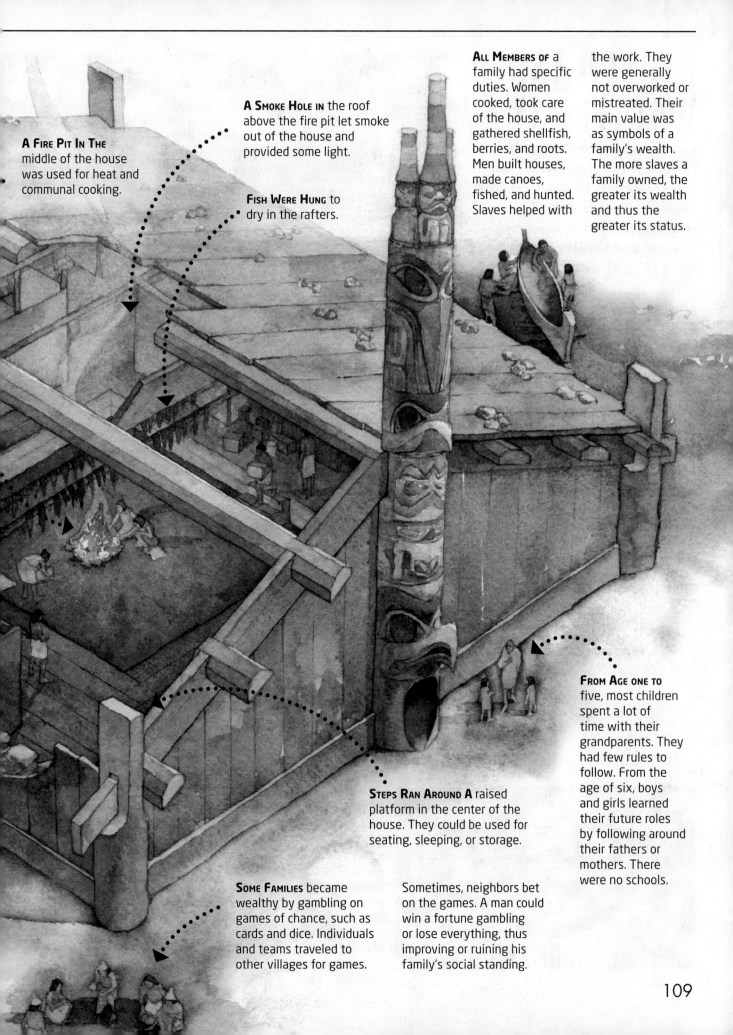

A SMOKE HOLE IN the roof above the fire pit let smoke out of the house and provided some light.

A FIRE PIT IN THE middle of the house was used for heat and communal cooking.

FISH WERE HUNG to dry in the rafters.

ALL MEMBERS OF a family had specific duties. Women cooked, took care of the house, and gathered shellfish, berries, and roots. Men built houses, made canoes, fished, and hunted. Slaves helped with the work. They were generally not overworked or mistreated. Their main value was as symbols of a family's wealth. The more slaves a family owned, the greater its wealth and thus the greater its status.

FROM AGE ONE TO five, most children spent a lot of time with their grandparents. They had few rules to follow. From the age of six, boys and girls learned their future roles by following around their fathers or mothers. There were no schools.

STEPS RAN AROUND A raised platform in the center of the house. They could be used for seating, sleeping, or storage.

SOME FAMILIES became wealthy by gambling on games of chance, such as cards and dice. Individuals and teams traveled to other villages for games.

Sometimes, neighbors bet on the games. A man could win a fortune gambling or lose everything, thus improving or ruining his family's social standing.

CARVED AND WOVEN BEAUTY

Like artists everywhere, the people of the Northwest Coast used materials that were readily available to create art. The women excelled at weaving baskets and textiles. The men were skillful wood carvers.

▲ BASKETS WERE made from roots, twigs, and grasses. The materials were gathered and prepared in the summer for weaving in the winter. Roots and twigs were soaked, peeled, and split. Grasses were dried and dyed. Cedar bark and twigs were prized for baskets. Shiny bear grass and grape roots were often used to create designs on the finished baskets.

▼ WOOL FOR WEAVING was shorn from mountain goats and wool dogs, a breed raised by women especially for its thick fur. Chilkat (a division of the Tlingit) women used the wool of mountain goats to weave blankets that also served as ceremonial robes. Nuxalk women, of the Coast Salish group, pounded cedar-bark strips and wove them into ceremonial aprons, which they decorated with embroidery and beads, and sometimes painted wooden masks.

➤ WOODEN MASKS were used in ceremonies. Part of an animal mask might be hinged so that when a string was pulled, it revealed the human face behind it. Some ceremonies included stories of animals that turned into humans.

➤ HOUSHOLD ITEMS, such as cooking and storage boxes, were made to be useful as well as beautiful.

◄ **A CANOE WAS** made from a large hollowed-out cedar log. The log was partially filled with water. Red-hot rocks were placed in the water to make it boil. The boiling water made the wood soft, so cross-pieces of wood could be added to push out the sides. After the water was removed, the wood dried and became stiff. The canoe could then be decorated.

◄ **THE PAINTED** wooden screen (upper half of photograph) in this whale house is nine feet high and eighteen feet long. It separates a Tlingit master's private living area from the rest of the house. The painting represents a raven, the master's clan animal. The round hole (center, bottom of screen) is the opening through which the master entered and left. Since the opening is in the belly of the raven, each time the master passed through, it was as if he were being reborn from his ancestors. This house no longer stands, but the spectacular artworks remain in Klukwan, Alaska, as cherished heirlooms.

◄ **SOME TOTEM** poles were memorials to a family's history and heritage. Others marked the graves of leaders. A coffin could be placed in a fork at the top, or ashes could be placed in a hidden opening. Some totem poles were entrances to houses, with a hole for people to walk through. Some entrances were carved as ravens' beaks, with an arrangement of ropes and pulleys that let them open and close. The top figure in a totem pole represented the major animal associated with the owner's clan.

➤ **COPPERS WERE** thin sheets of decorated copper. They symbolized a chief's wealth. Copper wasn't found on the Northwest Coast but was acquired through trade with inland groups or with outsiders after contact was established.

111

An important event, such as a wedding, the naming of a child, or a coming-of-age ceremony, was marked with a big feast called a potlatch. The word comes from the Chinook word meaning "to give away." To show his wealth and social standing, the person holding the potlatch gave elaborate gifts to all who attended. Families sometimes worked and saved for years to be able to throw a potlatch.

Come One, Come All

Outsiders Arrive

Russians were the first to record reaching the area, in 1741. In 1774, Spanish ships sailed up the Pacific Coast from Mexico and encountered the Haida. Britain sent Captain James Cook to claim a foothold in the area in 1778. Russia and Britain were mostly interested in trading for sea-otter fur. Eventually, Russian, British, and American traders competed for the fur trade. The people of the Northwest Coast were shrewd traders, and they were happy to exchange fur pelts for guns, iron, sugar, blankets, flour, and sails for their canoes. However, contact with the new arrivals brought disastrous results.

▲ **Outsiders Carried** diseases that had never before existed in the Americas. Since the people had never been exposed to these diseases, they had no immunities to them. Therefore, when one person caught a disease, it spread rapidly, wiping out whole communities. By some estimates, the Northwest Coast people lost 90 percent of their population between 1800 and 1900. Above is a Haida cemetery.

▼ **The Reduction** in population had a significant effect on Northwest Coast culture. Survivors of epidemics gathered together in combined villages. But this sometimes led to fierce competition for leadership titles in the new villages. Leadership had always been determined by wealth as expressed in potlatch giveaways. Trade had brought even more wealth into the area. So the competition for leadership took the form of more and more elaborate potlatches. In some cases, to show how great their wealth was, people destroyed goods instead of giving them to others.

▲ **Before Long,** the animals that the people had depended on for food had been hunted for fur almost to extinction. For food and other supplies, the people had to rely more and more on trading posts set up by the Russians, Spanish, and British. Traders kept increasing the price of needed supplies to force the people to provide more furs. Sometimes, the owners of trading posts refused to sell supplies or closed up and moved away. Many of the people starved.

▼ **THE GOVERNMENTS** of Canada and the United States supported the settlers and disregarded the rights of the Northwest Coast people. The governments set up reservations (called reserves in Canada). These tracts of land were usually located at winter villages. Any land not part of an established reservation was considered to belong to the government and open to settlement. Thus, the people were denied their right to the land they had roamed for centuries.

▲ **GOVERNMENT** agents tried to convince the people to live as European-Americans did. Christian missionaries tried to convert the people to their way of worshiping, insisting that the people give up their traditional way of life. Some children were sent to boarding schools, where they were punished if they spoke their language. In 1884, the Canadian government banned potlatches and secret dancing societies. Some people defied the ban and went to jail. Others continued them in the guise of Christmas parties or charitable giving. But many obeyed the law, in effect giving up their culture. The ban was not lifted until 1951.

◀ **TRADERS HAD NO** interest in taking land from the Northwest Coast people. But in the 1840s, settlers began to arrive, and they wanted land. Factories for canning fish were built on the best salmon rivers. Lumber companies began logging. Gold was discovered, and miners flocked to the area.

115

Northwest Coast Nations Today

Today, thousands of Native Americans live along the Northwest Coast, some in reservations or reserves, and others in cities and towns. The people in the same region who speak related languages are called a nation. Governed by chiefs and elders, the nations work to raise awareness of their traditions, languages, beliefs, and ceremonies. Several nations have their own schools. Their languages and way of life were nearly destroyed, but the people of the Northwest Coast have survived and are determined to flourish. In recent years, the population has increased, though the number of people speaking the native languages is small.

➤ **NORTHWEST COAST** people continue to fight for the right to their land and culture. They have also fought against racism and for their rights as citizens of the U.S. or Canada. In 1912, the Alaska Native Brotherhood was formed. By 1922, it had won the right to vote—two years before Native Americans in the continental U.S. In the late 1930s, the group started a movement to restore totem poles as a way to reclaim part of the people's heritage. In 1944, in the U.S., Native Americans formed the National Congress of American Indians. This group works to keep tribes and tribal life alive.

▼ **IN THE 1850s,** government treaties with Northwest Coast people guaranteed them the right to fish in their traditional fishing grounds. Over the years, commercial and sports fishers used and sometimes blocked access to traditional fishing areas. More recently, Native Americans trying to practice a traditonal way of life have come into conflict with environmentalists and animals-rights activists. In 1999, the Makah held their first whale hunt in 70 years and harpooned a gray whale from a canoe. Some criticized them for this. But other groups have defended Native Americans' rights to their traditional way of life.

▼ **IN THE 1960s,** Kwakwaka'wakw chief James Sewid wanted to restore the sense of community that people had when many families lived together. He and others decided to build a plank house for the community in Alert Bay, British Columbia. It opened in 1966. The house posts have carved totems of Thunderbird and Grizzly Bear and crests from local tribes. The front of the house shows a killer whale, or orca. Here, the people can come to immerse themselves in the art and culture.

▲ **Some of Today's** Northwest Coast artists work in traditional styles. Others use traditional elements to create brand-new styles. Bill Reid is a Haida artist. He has created small sculptures as well as full-size totem poles. *The Raven and the First Men* (above) shows the first people attempting to escape from a shell.

▲ **Some of the** people have revived the custom of potlatch. As in former times, a potlatch is a celebration. There is singing and dancing. New members are adopted into clans. People may be given new names to honor them. And as in the past, gifts are given, though today the gifts may include canned salmon, homemade jellies, and boxes of fruit.

▶ **Like Native** Americans all over the U.S. and Canada, people of the Northwest Coast enjoy attending powwows (a cultural gathering and dance celebration) and performing traditional dances.

When John Henry was a little babe,
  A-holding to his mama's hand,
Says, "If I live till I'm twenty-one,
I'm going to make a steel-driving man, my
babe,
I'm going to make a steel-driving man."

When John Henry was a little boy,
  A-sitting on his father's knee,
Says, "The Big Bend Tunnel on the C. & O.
  Road
Is going to be the death of me, my babe,
Is going to be the death of me."

John he made a steel-driving man,
  They took him to the tunnel to drive;
He drove so hard he broke his heart,
  He laid down his hammer and he died, my
  babe,
  He laid down his hammer and he died.

O now John Henry is a steel-driving man,
  He belongs to the steel-driving crew,
And every time his hammer comes down,
  You can see that steel walking through, my
  babe,
  You can see that steel walking through.

The steam drill standing on the right-hand
  side,
  John Henry standing on the left;
He says, "I'll beat that steam drill down,
  Or I'll die with my hammer in my breast,
  my babe,
  Or I'll die with my hammer in my breast."

He placed his drill on the top of the rock,
  The steam drill standing close at hand;
He beat it down one inch and a half
  And laid down his hammer like a man, my
   babe,
  And laid down his hammer like a man.

John Henry

Traditional American Folk Song

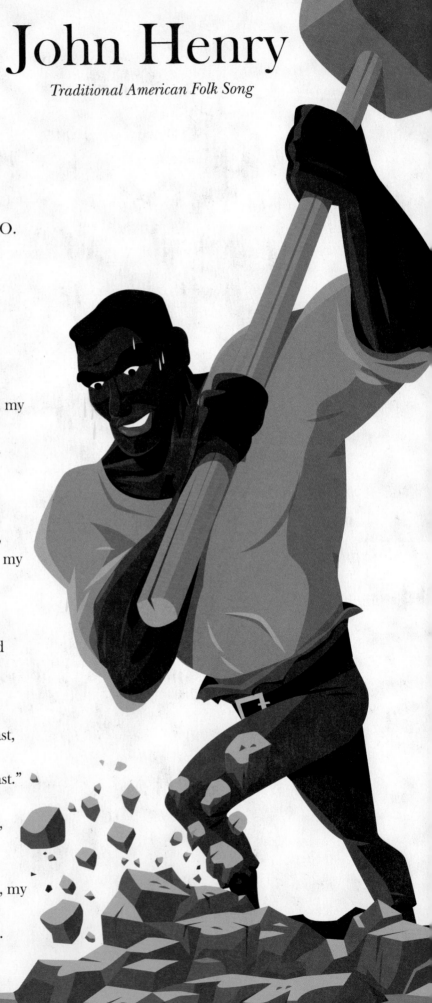

Johnny looked up to his boss-man and said,
    "O boss-man, how can it be?
For the rock is so hard and the steel is so tough,
I can feel my muscles giving way, my babe,
I can feel my muscles giving way."

Johnny looked down to his turner and said,
    "O turner, how can it be?
The rock is so hard and the steel is so tough
That everybody's turning after me, my babe,
That everybody's turning after me."

They took poor Johnny to the steep hillside,
    He looked to his heavens above;
He says, "Take my hammer and wrap it in
    gold
And give it to the girl I love, my babe,
And give it to the girl I love."

They took his hammer and wrapped it gold
And gave it to Julia Ann;
And the last word John Henry said to her
Was, "Julia, do the best you can, my babe
Was, "Julia, do the best you can."

"If I die a railroad man,
    Go bury me under the tie,
So I can hear old Number Four,
    As she goes rolling by, my babe,
    As she goes rolling by."

"If I die a railroad man,
Go bury me under the sand,
With a pick and shovel at my head and feet
And a nine-pound hammer in my hand,
my babe,
And a nine-pound hammer in my hand."

Back to Nature

by Marilyn Singer

We cover the earth
    with asphalt
        tarmac
        concrete
        brick
We want to be far away
    from humus
        moss and leaf mold
    from things soft and unpredictable
        that slide beneath our feet
But even in the city
    sparrows nest in lampposts
        tree trunks rise from sewers
    and mulberries fat and purple
        rain on sidewalks
    turning the pavement soft and unpredictable
        making it slide beneath our feet

RING AROUND THE WORLD

by Annette Wynne

Ring around the world

Taking hands together

All across the temperate

And the torrid weather.

Past the royal palm-trees

By the ocean sand

Make a ring around the world

Taking each other's hand;

In the valleys, on the hill,

Over the prairie spaces,

There's a ring around the world

Made of children's friendly faces.

MIDWEST TOWN

by Ruth De Long Peterson

Farther east it wouldn't be on the map—
    Too small—but here it rates a dot and a name.
In Europe it would wear a castle cap
    Or have a cathedral rising like a flame.

But here it stands where the section roadways meet.
    Its houses dignified with trees and lawn;
The stores hold *tête-à-tête* across Main Street;
    The red brick school, a church—the town is gone.

America is not all traffic lights,
    And beehive homes and shops and factories;
No, there are wide green days and starry nights,
    And a great pulse beating strong in towns like these.

Text

"Fragile Frogs." Excerpts from *The Frog Scientist* by Pamela S. Turner. Text copyright © 2009 by Pamela S. Turner. Photographs copyright © 2009 by Andy Comins. Reprinted by permission of Houghton Mifflin Harcourt Publishing Company. All Rights Reserved.

Movers and Shapers by Patricia Macnair. Copyright © 2004 by Patricia Macnair. Used by permission of Macmillan Publishers Ltd.

"Spider," from *Every Thing On It by Shel Silverstein*. Copyright © 2011 by Evil Eye Music, Inc. Used by permission of HarperCollins Publishers and Edite Kroll Literary Agency Inc on behalf of the Silverstein Estate.

"The Frog," from *Cautionary Verses* by Hilaire Belloc. Reprinted by permission of Peters Fraser & Dunlop (www.petersfraserdunloop.com) on behalf of the Estate of Hilaire Belloc.

"Go Southward, Birds!" Reprinted with the permission of Scribner Publishing Group from *Summer Green* by Elizabeth Coatsworth. Copyright 1948 Macmillan Publishing Company; copyright renewed © 1976 Elizabeth Coatsworth Beston.

"Go Southward, Birds!" Reprinted by permission of Catherine Barnes.

"Go Southward, Birds!" Reprinted by permission of Elizabeth Gartner.

"The Jellyfish and the Clam," excerpted from *Bone Poems*. Copyright © 1997 by Jeff Moss. Used by permission of Workman Publishing Co., Inc, New York. All Rights Reserved.

"The Jellyfish and the Clam," from *Bone Poems*. Copyright © 1997 by Jeff Moss. Reprinted by permission of International Creative Management, Inc.

"Skeletons," from *All the Small Poems and Fourteen More* © Copyright 1987 by Valerie Worth. Illustrations © by Natalie Babbitt. Reprinted by permission of Henry Holt & Company, LLC. All Rights Reserved.

"To the Skeleton of a Dinosaur in the Museum," copyright © 1979 Lilian Moore. Used by permission of Marian Reiner.

"Pecos Bill," from *American Tall Tales* by Mary Pope Osborne.

"John Henry," from *American Tall Tales* by Mary Pope Osborne.

How the Stars Fell Into the Sky by Jerrie Oughton, illustrated by Lisa Desimini. Text copyright © 1992 by Jerrie Oughton. Illustrations copyright (c) 1992 by Lisa Desimini. Used by permission of Houghton Mifflin Harcourt Publishing Company. All Rights Reserved.

"Northwest Coast Peoples," from *Kids Discover*, 17(2). Copyright © 2007. Reprinted by permission of Kids Discover.

"John Henry (traditional song)," from *American Folk Poetry*.

"Back to Nature." © Marilyn Singer, from *Footprints on the Roof: Poems about the Earth*, Knopf, 2002.

"Legends" by Avis Harley from *The Poetry book: Sky Magic*, compiled by Lee Bennett Hopkins; Dutton Children's Books.

"A Birch Bark Canoe", from *Down to the Sea in Ships* by Philemon Sturges. Copyright © 2005 by Philemon Sturges, text. Used by permission of G.P. Putnam's Sons, a division of Penguin Group (USA) LLC.

Illustrations

16, 17 Andreas Peterson, Robert Islas, Brandon Cody

18, 19 Rajeev at KJA-Artists

20, 21, 22, 24, 25, 26, 27, 29 Andreas Peterson, Robert Islas, Brandon Cody

30, 31 Rajeev at KJA-Artists

45 Tamsin Hinrichsen

48 Olga Demidova

50 Scott Angle

118 Sebastiene Telleschi

121 Lindy Burnett

123 You Byun

Photographs

Photo locators denoted as follows: Top (T), Center (C), Bottom (B), Left (L), Right (R), Background (Bkgd)

14 (L) Hans Neleman/Getty Images, (BL) Britt Erlanson/Getty Images, (R) Hector Vivas/Getty Images; **15** (B) nobleIMAGES/Alamy, (L) Jorge Arciga/Newscom, (T) GJLP/ Science Source; **16** (L) Alfred Pasieka/Science Source, (C) POWER AND SYRED/Science Source; **17** (BC) Pietro M. Motta/Science Source, (T) Alfred Pasieka/Science Source, (BR) Scott Camazine/Getty Images; **18** (L) Dr. P. Marazzi/Science Source, (R) Alexander Tsiaras/Science Source, (C) © Tim Tadder/ Corbis; **19** Salisbury/Science Source; **20** Mehau Kulyk/Science Source; **21** (C) Edith Held/Corbis, (R) Taxi/Mike Owen; **22** (BL) Jeffery Allan Salter/Corbis SABA, (BR) Steve Gschmeissner/Science Source, (B) Scott Camazine & Sue Trainor/Science Source, (T) Roy McMahon/Corbis; **24** (L) Andriano/Shutterstock, (B) BSIP/UIG, (BL) Ed Reschke/Getty Images; **25** ONOKY - Photononstop / Alamy; **26** (B) ADRIENNE HART-DAVIS/Science Source; (T) Brian Stablyk/Getty Images; **27** (BL) pterwort/Shutterstock, (BR) Mega Pixel/Shutterstock, (B) Dave Roberts/Science Source; **28** (L) Alfred Pasieka/Science Source, (BR) James Cavallini/Science Source; **29** (BR) SHEILA TERRY/ Science Source; **30** (T) andi/Fotolia, (B) Science Source, (R) © Beyond Fotomedia GmbH/ Alamy; **31** (BR) DU CANE MEDICAL IMAGING LTD/Science Source, (CR) wavebreakmedia/ Shutterstock; **33** Universal Images Group Limited/Alamy; **34** Tom Gaffney/ZUMA Press/ Newscom; **36** Creative Jen Designs/Shutterstock; **37** (B) University of Leicester/Corbis, (T) David Warren/Alamy; **39** University of Leices/Demotix/Corbis; **40** Robbie Jack/Corbis; **41** DARREN STAPLES/Reuters/Corbis; **42** DARREN STAPLES/Reuters/Corbis; **43** (L) Antiques & Collectables / Alamy, (R) AFP/Getty Images; **44** travelib wales / Alamy; **46** (Bkgd) Sinelyov/Shutterstock, (T) Roger Tidman/Corbis; **47** (B) National Geographic / SuperStock, (T) Peter Chigmaroff/Wave/ Corbis; **103** Canadian Museum of Civilization/CORBIS; **107** (BL) Norma Lee Kayler photograph/ Robert H. Ruby, M.D. Papers (Ms 170), (BR) Edward S. Curtis/ Charles Deering McCormick Library of Special Collections, Northwestern University Library, (CL) Raymond Gehman/National Geographic, (C) Richard A. Cooke/Corbis, (CR) Werner Forman/Art Resource, (L) Edward S. Curtis/National Geographic, (R) Christopher Morris/Corbis; **110** (BL) The Bridgeman Art Library,(BR) Werner Forman/Art Resource, (C) Alaska State Library/Winter & Pond Photograph collection, (T) Courtesy of the Burke Museum of Natural History; **111** Seattle Art Museum, Gift of John Hauberg & John & Grace Putnam **115** (B) North Wind Pictures, (C) Culver Pictures / The Art Archive at Art Resource, NY, (T) Northwest Museum of Arts & Culture/Eastern WA State Historical Society, Spokane/Edgar Dowd; **116** (BL) Anthony P. Bolante/Sygma/Corbis, (CL) C. M. Archbold/Corbis, (C) Nick Didlik Photography, (T) Lawrence Migdale; **117** (C) Gunter Marx/ Corbis, (R) Bob Rowan/Progressive Image/Corbis; (T) Mike Zens/Corbis; **120** cdrin/Shutterstock; **122** Underwood Photo Archives / SuperStock; **124** Craig Aurness/Corbis.

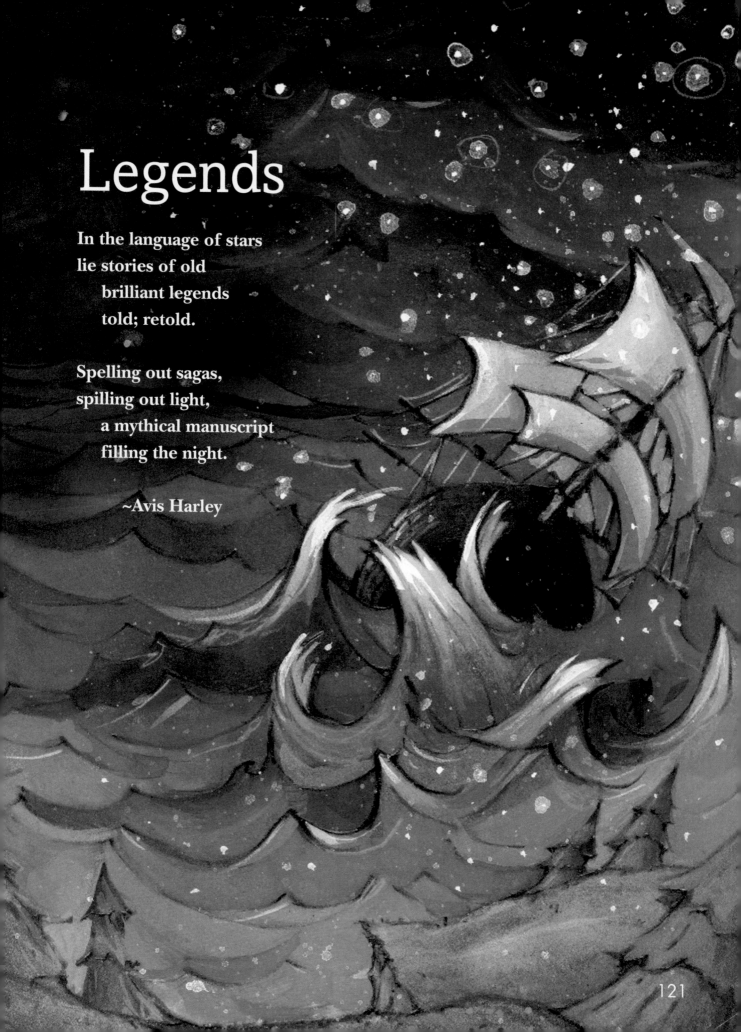

Legends

In the language of stars
lie stories of old
  brilliant legends
  told; retold.

Spelling out sagas,
spilling out light,
  a mythical manuscript
  filling the night.

      ~Avis Harley

A BIRCH BARK CANOE

by Philemon Sturges

If you wish to see the sea,
Build a sturdy boat like me
That's light and strong.
Then come along,
Follow river's winding way,
Watch herons stalk and beavers play.
Run the rapids, and then haul
Me round the waterfall.
And when, at last, the sea greets you,
Be grateful for your birch canoe.